AARP®

SUDOKU

TO

EXERCISE YOUR MIND

FRANK LONGO

Sterling Publishing Co., Inc.
New York

AARP Books include a wide range of titles on
health, personal finance, lifestyle, and other
subjects to enrich the lives of 50+ Americans.

For more information, go to www.aarp.org/books

AARP, established in 1958, is a nonprofit, nonpartisan organization
with more than 35 million members age 50 and older. The views
expressed herein do not necessarily represent the policies of AARP
and should not be construed as endorsements.

The AARP name and logo are registered trademarks of AARP,
used under license to Sterling Publishing Co., Inc.

2   4   6   8   10   9   7   5   3   1

Published by Sterling Publishing Co., Inc.
387 Park Avenue South, New York, NY 10016
© 2006 by Sterling Publishing Co., Inc.
Distributed in Canada by Sterling Publishing
$^{C}/o$ Canadian Manda Group, 165 Dufferin Street
Toronto, Ontario, Canada M6K 3H6
Distributed in the United Kingdom by GMC Distribution Services
Castle Place, 166 High Street, Lewes, East Sussex, England BN7 1XU
Distributed in Australia by Capricorn Link (Australia) Pty. Ltd.
P.O. Box 704, Windsor, NSW 2756, Australia

Sterling ISBN-13: 978-1-4027-4199-9
ISBN-10: 1-4027-4199-5

For information about custom editions, special sales, premium and
corporate purchases, please contact Sterling Special Sales
Department at 800-805-5489 or specialsales@sterlingpub.com.

CONTENTS

INTRODUCTION

To solve sudoku puzzles, all you need to know is this one simple rule:

Fill in the boxes so that each of the nine rows, each of the nine columns, and each of the nine 3×3 sections contain all the numbers from 1 to 9.

And that's all there is to it! Using this simple rule, let's see how far we get on this sample puzzle at right. (The letters at the top and left edges of the puzzle are for reference only; you won't see them in the regular puzzles.)

The first number that can be filled in is an obvious one: box EN is the only blank box in the center 3×3 section, and all the digits 1 through 9 are represented except for 5. EN must be 5.

The next box is a little trickier to discover. Consider the upper left 3×3 section of the puzzle. Where can a 4 go? It can't go in AK, BK, or CK because row K already has a 4 at IK. It can't go in BJ or BL because column B already has a 4 at BQ. It can't go in CJ because column C already has a 4 at CM. So it must go in AJ.

Another box in that same section that can now be filled is BJ. A 2 can't go in AK, BK, or CK due to the 2 at EK. The 2 at GL rules out a 2 at BL. And the 2 at CP means that a 2 can't go in CJ. So BJ must contain the 2. It is worth noting that this 2 couldn't have been placed without the 4 at AJ in place. Many of the puzzles rely on this type of steppingstone process.

We now have a grid as shown at right. Let's examine column A. There are four blank boxes in column A; in which blank box must the 2 be placed? It can't be AK because of the 2 in EK (and the 2 in BJ). It can't be AO because of the 2 in IO. It can't be AR because of the 2 in CP. Thus, it must be AN that has the 2.

By the 9's in AL, EM, and CQ, box BN must be 9. Do you see how?

We can now determine the value for box IM. Looking at row M and then column I, we find all the digits 1 through 9 are represented but 8. IM must be 8.

This brief example of some of the techniques leaves us with the grid at left. You should now be able to use what you learned to fill in CN followed by BL, then HL followed by DL and FL. As you keep going through this puzzle, you'll find it gets easier as you fill in more. And as you keep working through the puzzles in this book, you'll find it gets easier and more fun each time. The final answer is shown at right.

The puzzles in this book have the following difficulty levels: 1–50: beginner; 51–100: very easy; 101–150: easy; 151–200: medium; 201–250: medium-hard; 251–270: hard. Enjoy exercising your mind with these puzzles!

—Frank Longo

Sample puzzle (top right)

	A	B	C	D	E	F	G	H	I
J	4	2	1						
K	7	3	6		2		1	8	4
L	9	8	5		7		2		6
M	1	5	4	3	9	2	6	7	8
N	2	9			7	5	6		
O	5	7	6		1	4	8	9		2
P	3		2	4	6			8		5
Q	8	4	9			3			
R						4			

Grid (middle right)

	A	B	C	D	E	F	G	H	I
J	4	2	3	6	7	9	5	1	8
K	5	7	6	9	2	3	1	8	4
L	9	8	5	2	7	1	2	4	6
M	1	5	4	3	9	2		6	7	8
N	2	1	8	7	5	6			9
O	6	7	1	4	8	9	3	2
P	3	9	2	2	6		8		5
Q	8	4	9	5	3		7	6	
R	7	6	3	4		3			

Grid (bottom left)

	A	B	C	D	E	F	G	H	I
J	4	2			9				
K				2		1	8	4
L	9	8	5		7	1	2	3	6
M	1		4	3	9	2		7	8
N	2	9	8	7	5	6			
O		7		1	4	8	9		2
P	3		2		6		8		5
Q	8	4	9		3			1	
R									

Final answer (bottom right)

	A	B	C	D	E	F	G	H	I
J	4	2	1	6	8	3	5	9	7
K	7	3	6	5	2	9	1	8	4
L	9	8	5	4	7	1	2	3	6
M	1	5	4	3	9	2	6	7	8
N	2	9	8	7	5	6	4	1	3
O	6	7	3	1	4	8	9	5	2
P	3	1	2	9	6	7	8	4	5
Q	8	4	9	2	3	5	7	6	1
R	5	6	7	8	1	4	3	2	9

1

8	7	9	6	3	1	4	5	2
3	4	1	8	5	2	6	9	7
6	5	2	7	4	9	8	3	1
7	3	4	2	8	6	5	1	9
9	1	5	3	7	4	2	6	8
2	6	8	1	9	5	3	7	4
5	9	7	4	6	8	1	2	3
4	2	3	5	1	7	9	8	6
1	8	6	9	2	3	7	4	5

2

2	8	5	9	6	3	4	7	1
6	3	9	1	4	7	2	5	8
7	1	4	2	5	8	3	6	9
1	4	7	5	2	9	8	3	6
5	2	3	7	1	6	7	9	4
9	6	8	3	8	4	5	1	2
8	3	6	4	7	1	9	2	5
7	5	1	8	9	2	6	4	3
4	9	2	6	3	5	1	8	7

3

8	4	6	1	5	7	9	2	3
9	2	1	8	6	3	4	7	5
3	7	5	4	9	2	8	6	1
2						1	3	
	1			7			4	
	6	4						8
			5	3		2		
1		9			6	7	5	
4					9	3	8	

4

5	6					9		
4	7	3	2	1	5	6	8	9
2	3		4	6		7		8
6	9		5				6	
1	2							7
9	5			7		4		
3	8	1	6	7	4	3	2	9
8	1			8	3	2		
9	4	6					7	9

5

	1	2	3	4	5	6	7	8	9
A	2	9	8	4	1	5	3	6	
B	7	3	1	2	8	6	4	5	9
C	4	5	6	3	7	8			5
D	3	4			6	9		7	2
E	1	2			4			3	8
F	5	7		8	3				
G	6				9	4			
H	8		5	6	2		8		
I	9		2					1	6

6

6		8						4
		4		1				
			2	8	4		1	9
			1			5	3	
	8		5		6		2	
	2	6			9			
9	4		7	6	5			
			3			4		
8						7		3

Or blue? I like blue!

1238

Hello!

Do I like this pen? Or this one?

7

7	4	6	1	2	3	5	8	9
2	3	1	4	5	6	7	89	7
4	9	5	7	8	4	3	2	1
9		5	4	2	3	6	7	8
	7		1		8		2	
				9		4		6
1			3	7	5		9	
5						1		
						2	6	5

8

8	3	1	4	2	5	9	7	6
4	1	2	6	9	7		8	3
5	6	4	2	3	1	7	9	8
2	9	6	8	5	3	4	1	7
3	8	5	7	1	2	6	4	9
7	5	4	3	6	8	2	9	1
1	9	3	5	8	4	3	2	7
9	4	7	1	4	6	8	6	2
6	2	8	1	7	9	4	3	5

9

9	6	5	4	2	7	1	8	3
5	7	8	3	6	8	2	9	4
8	5	2	6	9	5	4	5	6
1	8	7	9	4	6	4	2	3
6	2	5		1	3	7	5	9
9	4	3	7		2	6	1	8
7	2	6	5	8	9	3	2	1
5	8	9	6	3	4	8	7	5
4	3	1	2	7	7	9	6	4

10

1	3	4			5			
8	6	2		9		3		
9	5	7		3				
6	8		4					
2			9		7			4
				3			2	8
			2			1	8	
		8	4				7	
			3			4	9	5

11

		3	5	6				
5				4	9	2		
	8	9						6
	3			5		9		
8			4		6			1
	7		2			8		
6					8	1		
		1	9	8				5
			1	3	4			

12

		5	6	3				9
	3	8		7				
			2			1		3
	6			1		3		
1	8						5	2
		4		8			1	
9		7			5			
			9			4	6	
3				2	1	7		

13

		4		1	9			
2	5	7						
		3		7				6
8	2				6		9	
9			7		3			5
	7		9				4	2
4				9		5		
						6	8	9
			6	8		7		

14

6					4		2	
	7		1			3	8	
		5		8	6			
2		6		9		4		
5								8
		8		2		9		1
			4	6		8		
	6	9			8		7	
	4		7					2

15

		3			2			9
9	4			6				
		1	9	8			5	4
8						3	1	
			8		5			
	7	4						8
1	5			7	9	6		
				1			8	5
6			3			1		

16

1		8	3		4			
			1	2			5	
	3			5				1
6	8					2		
3		7				6		8
		2					1	4
9				4			7	
	6			9	1			
			8		5	1		9

17

				1		2		
6	8	7	9					3
			4	3				5
					5	1	8	7
	1					5		
5	7	9	6					
2				7	9			
7					3	6	9	4
		1		6				

18

	6	7			5			
			3			6	4	2
	1		4					8
			2	7	8			
5	8						2	1
	9	6	1					
6				4		5		
8	3	4		5				
		9				2	8	

19

8			5	3				
7		1	4					
			9	7		5	8	
		8				5	3	
2	4						8	6
	1	3				9		
5	6		8	7				
				4	2			5
			9	2				1

20

			3			9	1	
		8			5		6	7
	7		1					8
7		4			2			
			8	4	7			
			9			2		4
3				9		4		
6	1		5			8		
	9	7		8				

10

3		7		4				
	2			3	1		8	
	5				9			6
		3			8	9		
7			5		2			8
		5	9			1		
6			3				1	
	9		2	8			6	
			5			7		9

3	7	5	9					
			7	8		1		
	2	8				6		
	6	9	3					
2			5		8			3
				4	9	8		
		7				8	5	
		6		7	1			
					9	3	1	7

			8	3	2	4		
3				4			2	
	4	7	1					
	2		5					9
8		9				1		2
7				9		6		
				8	9	1		
	6			7				8
		5	3	1	6			

		6			2		5	8
	1		3	5				
8	5			9				
		8				5	1	
5			4		9			6
	6	3				8		
			1				8	9
			6	5			2	
9	7		8			1		

25

6			5				8	
8	2				4	7		
		4	3					5
			5	8		6		
		7		9		3		
	6		2	1				
5					7	2		
		6	8				3	9
	4				9			7

26

	2	8	4		9			
			5	2				3
7		3						9
4				9			1	
	6	9				5	3	
	5			6				2
9						8		5
6			7	2				
			8		1	9	2	

27

2		7	3		8			
	3			9	6			
			7				9	1
	4					9		2
	5	2				8	7	
6		9					4	
1	7				5			
			4	7			3	
			1		2	7		4

28

9			3		2		4	
3			5			7		
		8		9			3	
8				2			7	
	3	7				6	8	
	9			3				1
	6			5		1		
		9			3			2
	2		7		9			8

2	7			1	8			
6		5				7		
			2				3	5
			8	2				4
	3	8				1	6	
7				3	6			
3	2				4			
		4				6		3
			6	8			4	9

		5		3		1		
2	8						4	
		3	5		4			
	4			2	8			7
3	1						2	6
7			1	9			5	
			9		5	7		
	7						3	8
		1		8		2		

6		4				8	7	
	8				4		3	
5		9			7			
			6	3				2
3				2				1
2			7	4				
			1			4		3
	6		5				2	
	7	8				6		9

6					1		3	9
2		3					7	
4	9			5				
			1		5	8		
		8		6		7		
		6	4		3			
			4				5	7
	2					6		1
5	7		2					4

3 3

9				2			8	
8	2					4		
	3		8	7	5			1
	5		4			9		
			6		3			
		4			1		5	
2		9	7	4			1	
		8					7	5
	7			3				4

3 4

	2		1		3			
	9					8	4	5
4		6		8				
		2	3					6
	8	3				9	2	
2			6	1				
			5			1		7
1	6	7				3		
			7		2		8	

3 5

		5			7	6		1
4	2				3			
			1	5		8		
5	6							7
		4		3		2		
7							6	9
	8		3	9				
			2				7	3
1		3	6			9		

3 6

5		4		3	6			
		3	9				4	
			5				3	9
9		7		5				
	8		4		3		6	
			1			2		8
3	1				5			
	5				4	1		
			2	9			3	6

	1		7			3		
		5		9				2
9	7		1		6			
	4			3		6		
6	8						3	5
		2		5			8	
			5		9		6	3
4				7		1		
		8			1		4	

2	6			7		4		
		1	9			7		
	4						6	3
			7	8				5
6			3		9			1
8				2	5			
7	2						5	
		4			7	8		
		3		9			7	2

5				8		2		7
1	2				4			
			2	9			6	
	5	1				9		
9			8		6			2
		2				8	7	
	8			4	2			
			1				8	3
3		9		6				5

		4	3					5
	3	8		6	7			
5						6		2
			3			9	5	
	9		4		2		6	
	8	1			6			
6		3						9
			7	9		3	1	
9				1		2		

4 1

	5	1			6		4	
			5	8				9
7		8			1			
	7		1			6		
5				4				2
		3			2		8	
			8			7		5
2				1	5			
	4		7			1	9	

4 2

9		3						4
			5	6	8			
6					3		7	2
		5		1		7	3	
	1						5	
	3	7		2		4		
3	6		7					9
			2	3	9			
1						3		5

4 3

	4			3		2		
		9	5		1		7	
2				7				9
3		2			4			
5	7						1	2
			7			6		8
6				1				5
	5		8		3	1		
		4		9			8	

4 4

	5	3				6		
	6		5		2			8
		9		6			5	
3			6					5
		1		2		4		
4					8			3
	4			1		3		
2			7		6		9	
		7				5	1	

4 5

			2				1	9
	4	7	3					
	8	1		5				
1	9				7			8
		6	1		3	7		
3			8				6	2
				3		9	8	
					6	3	4	
6	3				9			

4 6

1				8				6
	6	9				7		
					2	3		1
		6	5				7	3
	1			2		3		6
3	7				9	5		
9		7	8					
		1				9	8	
8			2					4

4 7

8			9	2				
				3	8	2	1	
	4			7	1			
6		4					8	5
		8			2			
5	3				4			6
			2	5			6	
7	8	9	4					
				1	9			8

4 8

			8				1	7
6			9	2			8	
	2	3				5		
		6	4					3
	3			1			9	
4				9	7			
		2				6	7	
	7		3	2				5
9	6			1				

49

			4	8			7	
7	9	4						
6			7	1	5			
			3	2	6	5		
2								1
9	8	6	2					
		2	6	5				4
						7	5	8
	3		4	8				

50

8	5			6				
4	2				5			
	7				8	2	9	
5				4	1			
		3		8		4		
		2	7					6
	9	8	3				7	
			4				1	8
				1			5	2

51

	1	8			7			
			2	9			5	
7			4	1	5			
		5				3	1	4
8								6
9	2	3				8		
			3	8	1			9
	8			5	4			
			9			7	3	

52

4	1		2					
			4			9		1
	7			1		5	6	
1				8	2			
6				2				8
		4	1					6
	5	1		6			7	
3		8			1			
				9			8	2

7		6					9	
		2	3	7				
		3	5					7
9	6				5		8	
2	3						7	5
	5		7				1	6
3				7	8			
			8	9	2			
	1					7		4

8	6	1	2					
		4		9				7
7	5			1				
			9		3		7	
2		6				9		3
	8		5		6			
			4				9	5
5			6			3		
					2	6	8	1

8	3			9	7		2	
	7	9	5					
2						9		7
			3	7		2		
		6				3		
		3		5	9			
1		4						8
				3	1	4		
	9		4	1			6	2

	3	4					7	
					7	9		6
9			8	2	3			
		8	9			1		
3	4						9	5
		9			6	4		
			6	9	4			1
6		2	1					
	7					6	5	

		7			9		6	
		5	1			8		
	8	3		2	6			5
	9			6				3
6								1
5				7			4	
2			3	4		7	1	
		9			7	5		
	1		6			4		

			4	6				1
6				5		2		
		2		9	8			4
		8					6	2
	6		8		9		4	
4	9					3		
7			6	2		4		
		6		1				9
1				8	7			

4			7			6	3	
		6		9	5			
	9			6		8		
8					3		6	
5				2				3
	2		1					8
		2		5			7	
			2	3		9		
	7	1			9			2

			1	5	7			2
7	5			9				
9		3				5		
	4	8			3			
	7						6	
			4			3	8	
		2				6		5
			6				9	8
6			9	1	4			

6 1

8						5	1	
	4	6		7				
			1			4	7	2
6		2			8			
		8	6			7	1	
			3			9		8
3	1	5			9			
				6		2	9	
	6	9						3

6 2

8	6	1	3					
4					6	5		
5	3		4					
	4			6	8			
		3	7		1	2		
			9	3			7	
				2			4	5
		6	5					9
					7	6	2	1

6 3

			6			8		5
	7		3				4	
		3		2			7	
4				6	9			2
3		8				9		4
6			4	3				8
	3			4		1		
	2				3		8	
9		4			8			

6 4

	7	3	8				2	
9					1		7	
1	4				9			
	7			6		4		
4		8				5		6
		5		4			1	
			5				6	8
	9		4					5
	5			3	6	2		

				2		4	6	
9		4	7					3
3		5					2	
2			9					
	8		2	4	6		9	
					3			4
	3					5		2
6					7	8		9
	7	9		1				

2						7		9
4			8	2		6		
	6			3	9	8		
	9		7				4	
		7				1		
	2				6		7	
		3	4	8			9	
		1		9	3			5
9		2						1

4		8					5	
	6				1			4
	9		8		3			6
				5			3	1
		2		6		9		
7	4			3				
3			7		2		1	
6			3				8	
	1					3		2

1		6			7		2	
7		5					8	
	2			1	6			
	4	7			1			
3				2				6
			5			7	1	
			2	8		3		
	9					8		2
	7		6			1		4

69

5				4		3		
7			6		9			
		2	7				1	
	2	1	4				3	
8								1
	5				6	7	4	
	4				1	2		
			5		2			9
		8		7				6

70

			7	1			3	6
	8	5				2		
		1		8			9	
2			3					8
	6		1		9		2	
5				8				1
	9			4		5		
		6				4	7	
3	4			9	6			

71

2	3		7				4	
		9		6				8
				8	9			7
9	2	5						
	4		5		2		7	
						2	5	6
8		3	1					
6				9		7		
	9				4		6	5

72

1	3	5						
				1	3	7	5	
		7	5					2
			4		6		1	
6								7
	2		8		7			
7					9	4		
	8	4	6	7				
						5	7	3

23

73

	2				9		5	7
			1	8			2	
9				6		8		
4					5	2		
5		9				3		8
		3	8					5
		6		5				3
	5			4	8			
8	4		9				1	

74

9			5	4	3			
	6			1				3
			8			9	1	
	9					8	7	
		5		8		2		
	1	7					9	
	3	2			5			
4				2			5	
			4	6	1			7

75

4			7	9			6	
		6		3			5	4
5	9				1			
1		7				8		
			2		4			
		2				4		9
			5				4	8
2	6			1		5		
	7			4	9			3

76

5	9	7						
		2	9			8		
		4			2		9	7
9	1							
2			5	4	1			7
							8	1
	6	9		1			4	
			7		6	8		
						1	6	3

2			5				1	
	7		3	1	9	6		
9	5					8		
3					6	1		
		9				4		
		2	7					5
		7					3	8
		8	2	3	5		4	
	4				8			9

		8	6		9			
	6	4		7				
9	7				8		1	4
3		9						
7			1		3			9
						7		6
4	2		8				6	1
			1			2	4	
			4		5	3		

	9						5	8
7				9		3	1	
			1	2	8			
			7	5		4		
1	5						8	7
			3			8	1	
				6	2	9		
	8	9		4				6
3	1						2	

	7			1	8			2
1				6	3			
		4		5		6		
				2			3	
8	3		5		1		4	9
	2		9					
		3		8		7		
		8	6					5
6			4	2			8	

81

		9		7		6		
7			4				9	
	8				3	2		7
	3		7					
9	5						8	4
					4		1	
4		6	2			5		
	2				7			8
		8		4		3		

82

2				5				1
8		7			4			
4	5					6		
		2	5		8		6	
	1			3			9	
	8		6		7	3		
		8					2	6
			9			8		5
9				2				4

83

8	9	1			6		3	
		7		1	3			
						8	5	
3			1					
1	7		9		2		4	6
				4				2
	1	8						
			7	4		6		
	4		2			9	1	7

84

3				2	5			1
	5		6	1				
8	1					2		
		9	2					6
	4	8				1	5	
6				7	9			
		1					4	9
			4	6			1	
4			3	9				8

85

4						3	8	2
6			9				7	
		2		4	1			
8				2		5		
	9		1		6		3	
		1		5				9
			4	1		7		
	5				3			8
7	6	8						3

86

4	7		8					3
	6			2		7		
3		5		6	4			
	1				8			
9		4				8		1
			5				4	
			9	5		4		7
		7		8			3	
5					2		1	9

87

				3	6			9
	2	8			9	7		
3		5		8				
	3				4			
2	5		8		7		9	4
			3				5	
				4		1		2
		1	6			8	4	
5			1	7				

88

		7		9				8
	4			2	7			5
	1	9			5			
7				6	5			
4	2						6	1
		1	9					2
			5			2	7	
9			8	6			3	
6				7		8		

89

1	2						8	
			3	4				2
	5	7		1		9		
	9		4					
2		8	7		5	4		6
				3		5		
		9		6		2	7	
6			9	5				
	3						9	8

90

		9			6		8	
	1		2			9		
4		7		9			3	
5	6		3					
9		4				7		3
			1				5	6
	4		6			3		8
	2		9			5		
	9		3			1		

91

5			1				3	
2				3			8	
	4	3	2					
		6			7			8
4		9		5		3		7
7			4			9		
					5	4	6	
	1			4				3
	8				3			1

92

8				1	5			
	6		9				2	3
	3	4						1
		3				2	8	
			4	8	7			
	9	8				4		
2						5	3	
6	8				9		4	
			1	2				9

6	9		3					
4		3		2			8	
		2				4		1
1			9	8				
	3		2		7		9	
			3	4				2
3		5				8		
	7			5		1		4
					8		5	9

			9	5	4			
	2		1	8				4
9	5	4						
6	9					2		
1		7				4		6
		2					9	8
						6	7	3
7			9	3		2		
			7	6	2			

	3		8		1			
		9		5		8		
7	4						5	
		2	4			5		9
9				2				1
6		1			7	3		
	2						1	5
		7		4		6		
			5		3		4	

9	3							2
	8	2		4	6			
		6	9					5
4	1		2	6				
		7				4		
			8	5			3	1
3				4	9			
		8	7			2	5	
5							1	3

6	7			3				
3		9				6	7	5
			7	1				
					8		3	9
		5	4		7	8		
1	9		5					
			7	9				
5	2	7				9		1
			5				4	7

			2	6			8	
1				3	5			
8		2	4	1				
	2	4		3		8		
9								1
		1		8		3	6	
			4	6	9			3
	9	7						8
	7			9	8			

	4	5	9					
				3	2			
9		2		1			5	3
5	8				4			9
			7		2			
4			5				8	6
8	5			4		6		1
		6	3					
					5	8	3	

			9	3		8		1
	4	7			1			
9	1							2
			6	4	1			9
	8					5		
2		1	7	5				
3							1	5
			2			7	9	
6		4		9	5			

101

3		8			9			
	9		4		1			
				6		4		
9			6					4
2	3						6	5
8					2			9
		1		4				
			8		6		1	
			7			8		6

102

	7			8		9		
8					9	7	5	4
		3			6		2	
		7	3					
5		6					4	8
				4	1			
	3		4			6		
7	1	5	8					3
		4		1			8	

103

7	5					3		
2			8					
			5			4	8	
	7		6	9		5		
5		9		2		8		7
		2		4	5		1	
	6	5			9			
				3				5
		1					3	8

104

			4				6	
4					7			1
5	6			9	8	3		
		6					4	
1			9					6
	2				1			
	7	9	3				5	2
2			6					3
	3			8				

105

	1			3	5			
4		5	1					6
2	9	3						
			6		3		1	
		9				4		
	4		9		7			
						1	8	5
1					4	9		2
			8	2			7	

106

4	8		7		9		3	
		5		8			9	4
		9		1		2		
2				7				
			4		1			
				3				6
		2		6		3		
9	1			4		6		
	4		9		2		7	1

107

6		4		8	1			
	3	7						
		2	9	3				
1					5	7	6	9
	7						8	
5	4	6	8					2
			6	4	8			
						3	4	
			3	9		5		7

108

			3	6	7			
	7	2			4		9	1
			1			6		8
4				5				
	5	9				8	2	
			7					4
9		6		2				
1	2		4			5	6	
			9	3	6			

	2					4		3
3	6	9	2					1
				8		2		
	9	1	5					
			7	2	8			
				3	8	6		
		7		6				
6					2	9	1	4
1		2					7	

		7		6		3	4	
	4	9		1				
6				8	2			
			6		3		8	
1	6						2	4
	2		7		1			
		2	9					7
			7			8	9	
	9	1		3		5		

4			8		3			
	7			9	6			
	2		5			9	3	
2							1	5
		4	6		8	2		
1	8							4
	4	6			1		9	
			9	6			4	
			2		5			6

	3		6		9	5		
	7	5			4			3
4				2			1	
2	4							
		9		5		1		
							4	2
	9			3				8
6				2		7	3	
		3	7		5		6	

113

	2		1					
	6						1	
1		7		6		5		2
3					5		2	1
		2				8		
4	7		2					9
5		6		7		1		3
	8						7	
					6		9	

114

8				5	6			
			2			1		
		1			9	4	6	
9		6		7				
	3			8			4	
			9			6		5
	4	3	5			7		
		2			1			
			8	7				3

115

1			8					2
				4		5		7
	8		2				1	
3		8			5	9		
	5						6	
		4	7			1		5
	1				9		5	
4		3		6				
5					1			6

116

7	4			6				
1			3					
	9			8	2			3
3		6				1		
	1			2			3	
		9				2		6
5			8	3			1	
				5				7
			4				6	5

117

			1				3	2
	8		3		9			4
	3		4	2				
3			5				6	8
		5				1		
7	4				1			3
			5	4		8		
8			9		7		2	
5	6				3			

118

		6			4			7
3		8			6		1	
	7		9					
		4	8	6				2
		9	7		3	6		
7				4	1	9		
					7		9	
	9			6			8	5
1				3			7	

119

	2					6		4
	4		5			1		
7					6	8		
	5			8	4			
		7	1		9	3		
			7	5			8	
		9	3					6
		2			5		9	
4		5					3	

120

		8	7	6				
6	7			9	4		5	
4		1					3	
	6			8				
	7		1		2			
		5				1		
	1				6		7	
	5		9	8		4	3	
			3	1	5			

121

9			2	3	1			
		7	4					1
1	2						9	
		4		1			7	8
	6						1	
8	1			5		3		
	8						2	9
6					4	8		
			9	7	8			4

122

	5	7	9					
				7		3		
	6			1	4			2
9						6		4
	4			9			2	
7		3						8
2			1	8			9	
		5		4				
					3	4	1	

123

	9	7		8			5	
3				4		8		
				6	3	9		
	5	9				1	4	
			4		8			
	6	2				7	8	
		6	2	9				
		8		7				5
	1			5		6	7	

124

		4	1		7			
5	6					3		
7					5			
	5			9		2		
1	2						8	9
		7		6			5	
			2					4
		1					9	5
			7		3	1		

125

	2		9				4	
		3		4				7
	8	4	6					1
3		1	4					
8	7						1	9
					9	3		2
6					4	1	2	
2				3		6		
	4				8		7	

126

6	4		1	3			5	
		5					1	9
					8			
		2			6	9	8	7
			8					
3	6	8	7			1		
			8					
4	7					2		
	5			1	2		4	3

127

					6		8	
	1							5
	2	8	1	7		6		4
		9			8	7		
2								3
		1	7			4		
8		3		1	7	5	9	
9							7	
	6		3					

128

4				9		1		3
	3				2		9	
	9	5		7				
	4		6		3			
		8		4		9		
			8		9		1	
			6			4	5	
	5		1				2	
1		2		5				8

2						8	3	
3			5	6				
		6	3					7
		7	1			9		
	2	3				1	5	
		1			8	6		
4					6	2		
				2	9			8
	6	2						9

		1		2		3		
			5				8	
4	9	3			8			2
9				4			7	6
			8		3			
2	4			1				8
8			4			6	1	3
	5				6			
		2		8		4		

2	8		5	7				
		5			4	8		
3				8	9		7	
5	3							
8		1				2		7
							8	6
	4		9	5				8
		8	3			1		
				1	8		6	2

		6	2		4			5
	7		9	8				
	2	5						3
6			1					7
	3			5			6	
7				9				2
2						3	9	
				4	2		7	
4			3			1	5	

	7	6					4	
				6		1		8
2			4			9		
				4	2	8	5	
9								1
5	1	8	3					
		9			7			3
8		7		1				
	3					7	1	

1	7		4				8	
		2		8				7
			7			2		4
	6			1				2
			9		8			
8				5			1	
4		5			6			
6				9		5		
	9				5		7	1

	5		7	6		4		
		2		8			5	
9			1				6	
	8	6			2			
5		9				2		6
			6			5	3	
	9				6			7
	6			7		9		
		4		5	1		8	

4		6	1					
8				2				6
		1	5			2	7	
		9	6				2	
	8						5	
	1				5	4		
	5	3			4	7		
1				3				5
					2	3		1

137

	5	7				6		
2			6	5	1		7	
			7				3	
5				4				
7		1		6		9		3
				9				8
	1				4			
	7		2	1	3			9
		2				3	4	

138

1		8		5			6	
	9			8			5	2
7		5			3			
8			7					
4		6				1		7
					6			3
			1			5		9
3	8			2			7	
	7			9		8		6

139

			5		7	3	4	
8			9	4				
5				3	1			
	9					7		
3		4		2		6		5
		7				2		
			1	7				4
			6	3				1
	1	8	2		4			

140

5	4			7				
	9		2			8	7	
		8				6		
	3		9		8			
		4		5		2		
			6		7		8	
		6				1		
	7	9			3		5	
				9			2	6

40

1 4 1

				8			3	7
		6	2	1				
8			6		7			
2	6	9					5	
		4				1		
	8					9	2	6
			1		8			2
			6	2	3			
3	7			5				

1 4 2

		1					2	6
3		7						
			5		1		8	9
			9	7				5
6	7		4		8		1	2
8			1	2				
1	6		7		9			
						6		7
7	4					1		

1 4 3

			1		4			5
			6			9	1	
		1	7	9	3			
	4						2	3
9								8
8	2						6	
		9	3	8		6		
	7	2		1				
3			2		6			

1 4 4

9				4			1	6
	3	6				5		
6						8		
	3		2	4			8	
		8				9		
	6			3	7	2		
		2						3
		5			3	1		
3	7		4					8

145

7	6							2
	8					4		
			4	2				1
5				1		6	9	
		7	2		9	8		
	1	8		7				4
8				5	7			
		9					7	
2							6	3

146

3	4			1				
	2					1	7	
		5		4				8
			2				1	7
8			4	7	9			5
2	5		8					
7			6			5		
	3	9					2	
			5				4	1

147

5			7	4				
	1	8					3	
			3	7				1
	7		8	3				
9		2				1		3
				2	1		6	
4				8	5			
	2					9	7	
					4	3		8

148

		4		9	2		8	
6	7	2						
		9	6	5				7
9			3					
8	2						7	4
					5			9
5				4	1	8		
						5	9	1
	9			5	8	7		

149

2	5				7		9	
	7				4	8		3
					1			6
9				7				
			9		6			
				2				5
1			3					
3		8	4				5	
	9		7				8	4

150

1			4		5			
	5			2			3	
4		8						2
6			2		9	1		5
			4					
8		9	3		1			4
2						9		8
	9			8			7	
			5		2			6

151

	3	9	2			6		
	6				8			
1				9			5	
	9	3		1				
6				3				1
				6		9	7	
	1			4				6
			5				4	
		2			6	7	3	

152

1							9	
	5		9		3		1	
	3			1		5		8
6				4				9
		8		3		6		
7			1					5
3		2		9			8	
	4		2		1		5	
	8							7

153

					5	1		
		4	8			2		
				6	2			7
8	1				6		7	9
9	7		4				1	2
3			5	9				
		5			3	9		
		8	7					

154

7			9	4		1		
1	2			6				
		4	3				7	6
8			2		9			
	7						8	
			1		8			7
2	5				7	4		
			6				9	1
	4		9	3				8

155

		1	2				8	4
			6			9		1
		7			3	5	2	
				4	6			
8	9						6	7
			9	7				
	1	8	5			2		
4		3			9			
6	2					1	4	

156

3								
	1	5	4				8	
		2		3			5	
1			3	6			9	
		3		8		2		
	9			2	7			8
	7			1		6		
	6				5	3	4	
								9

157

					1			
	4	2			7	8		3
	5				9			
	3							9
9		1	3	8	5	4		2
6						8		
			5				4	
5		8	9			7	3	
			1					

158

	1	3		6	4			
		9	3		8			
	5	7	9					
		8				1		3
9	3						6	2
5		1				9		
					1	8	4	
		8			7	6		
		5	4			3	2	

159

2		4		5				
9	8		6			2		
5						8		
1	4			9	2		6	
				7				
	6		8	1			9	5
	2							7
	5				3		4	9
				4		8		2

160

	1				5	9	3	
		3	7		2	4		
	5	2	4					
	2	1						
	4	9				7	8	
						2	1	
					6	5	7	
		5	3		4	6		
	9	4	5				2	

161

	3	4			5	2	6	
9	8							1
			2					
				9		7		
	4		6	7	8		1	
	6		1					
				2				
7							8	9
	1	6	8			7	3	

162

9		6			2	3		
				8				
3		2						6
				4			3	7
	2		3		8		6	
4	1			6				
1						7		4
				2				
		5	7			8		1

163

					6	2	5	
				1	7	6		
6		9						7
9				7		4	6	
		4				7		
	2	8		6				3
8						5		9
		1	6	2				
	9	3	8					

164

		6		4	9		5	
8				3		6		
4			5			9		2
	7			5				
6	5						3	1
				7			6	
2		4			5			6
		9		1				5
	1		3	2		4		

46

165

5	7		3			6		
	4					2	8	
		2		1	6			
			4			1	6	
1								9
	6	4			8			
			5	7		8		
	1	5					4	
		3			1		7	5

166

		8	7	1		9		4
6	9			4				3
		1	9			2		6
8								1
7		2			4	8		
9				3			2	7
3		5		9	2	1		

167

		8	2			3	9	
	4							1
3				8		2		7
				8	6			
	2		7	4	6		1	
		4	1					
4		9		6				3
8							2	
	1	7			3	5		

168

4	7		9			8		
8				4			2	
2	1							
			8	6	3	9		
			3					
	6	3	4	7				
							4	7
	5		6					9
		7			8		3	5

	9							
			7	2			3	8
7			8			5		
	5			7		9		
		2		8		4		
		4		5			7	
		6			2			9
1	2			6	7			
							5	

					7			1
	7		1	6	3			
	3					4		
7			3			1		6
	1		4			9		
6		9	2					3
	4					6		
			8	5	4		1	
9			3					

	7	2						1
3		5	4					
				1	6	2		
		3	8	4		6		
	2							3
		7		2	3	5		
		8	9	6				
					4	3		8
2						7	4	

2	1	4						
	7				2			
		5		6	9			
	8					5	9	
			2	3	9			
	4	7					1	
		6	3			4		
		7					2	
						1	6	9

Puzzle 173:

	4			2	8	1	7	
7			6		4		3	
		8			5			
	1							
4								8
						6		
			9			7		
	6		5		1			3
	7	2	4	3			1	

Puzzle 174:

9	7			8			3	
			5					1
		8				4		
2	1	6	3					
4								2
				2	6	7		8
		1				8		
8				7				
	9			2			6	5

Puzzle 175:

4					1			
		1		5			2	
9	6		3					
		5				4	6	2
		9				7		
2	1	7				5		
				9			4	1
	8			7		6		
			6					5

Puzzle 176:

		9		3			4	
	7			4	5			
4		2			6			9
	1						9	4
	9	7				3	6	
3	2						1	2
9			3			1		
			2	8			5	
	3			1		4		

				8	4			
		6		3		7	2	
	7		9		5	6		
		6				2	1	
	9	3				7		
	2	1		3			5	
6	5		8		7			
		9	4					

3			2	1		8		
				5			9	2
		9	7					
		2						5
		6	4	8	5	1		
1						4		
					4	7		
6	8			2				
		4			9	6		3

3	5	7		2		4		
		8						3
	2		3	1				
2		1					6	
			4					
	8					5		9
			3	2		9		
7						3		
		2		9		6	7	4

				3			8	
				5		4		
3	8	1		4		7		
1		6						4
4			2		5			1
9						2		3
		2		8		9	1	7
	9			3				
8			7					

181

5				1				
		7				2	3	4
2					3			
	2		3			6		5
		5		7		4		
6		8			4		9	
			6					8
9	4	3				5		
				4				9

182

	6	4					8	
		5			8			
		9	3			2		4
				6				1
7	2	3		1		8	6	5
6				8				
3		2			4	1		
			2			6		
	9					4	7	

183

	4		2					
		2			6	5	7	
	8					3		
			4	5	3	6	8	
	3	1	6	9	8			
		9					3	
	2	6	9			4		
					4		6	

184

			9		1			4
	8		5			1		6
					2	7	3	
		9				6		7
			4					
7		3				2		
	6	8	2					
9		5				3		1
3			4		8			

185

								6
		2	9		7		8	5
6					4		2	
	4		7			1	9	
		1				7		
	6	8			3		4	
	8		6					7
4	7		2		5	8		
5								

186

					2			9
1	8							
2					3	7		6
	7			3		2		1
3			8		6			7
8		2		7			3	
6		9	2					5
						9	2	
7			4					

187

					4		3	
4	9				3		2	1
			8					
5				7			1	2
	2	4	1		5	8	6	
8	7			6				5
				2				
2	4		6				8	3
	1		5					

188

5	2	8	3		1			7
	3	9	6					
							5	
1			7					
9	7						6	3
				6				9
	5							
					4	7	3	
7			9		3	4	1	8

52

	2			3				
	5		2			8		
	3		8		4	7		
	4		3	1				5
			4		9			
1				8	2		3	
		2	1		8		5	
		8			5		9	
				9			7	

3								8
			8				3	4
5				4		7	2	
	1					8	5	7
			4					
	5	3	9				1	
	7	5	2					1
9	8			1				
1								7

2	1	6			4			
8			1					6
				2		1		
	7	9		4				
6			7		1			5
				6		7	2	
		4		1				
3					6			2
			4			5	7	1

	4	8						
					6	4	2	3
					1			
4	2		9	7			6	1
				1				
1	5			3	2		9	7
			2					
6	7	1	3					
						9	7	

193

4	7			3				
		3	5		8	1	9	
		5						
		7		4	5		2	
9			1		6			7
	3		9	8		6		
						9		
	9	1	8		2	5		
				5			6	1

194

2				9				8
		8		2	7			9
	5						2	
	7				4		9	2
				3				
1	2		7				4	
	6						8	
3			2	8		7		
8				5				3

195

	2	7			6	5		
6						7	8	
9					7			6
	8	9			2			
			9	3	5			
			7			9	6	
2			5					3
	1	5						2
			3	6		1	4	

196

2						3	4	
		6	2	8			7	
7		8			9			
6						8		
	2		8	9	6		1	
		7						3
			3			1		9
	7			1	8	2		
	8	3						6

197

		5		2	6	3		
	8		9					6
3	1		8					
1		9			8			
	4						2	
			2			9		3
					2		9	4
5					9		3	
		8	5	4		6		

198

		6		1				
	2	5				7		
	3	7			4			9
			6				7	
		8	3		5	6		
	6				8			
8			7			4	3	
		3				2	8	
				8		5		

199

1				8		7	3	
5	6			4				
2		3						4
		1		2		4		
7	5						1	6
	4		1			5		
4						2		5
				2			6	3
	2	9		5				1

200

					7		9	
		9				8	6	
2			6	8				5
				6		2		7
3								1
5		4		7				
4				9	5			6
	1	3				7		
	5		7					

55

201

				5			8	
4	1							6
6		7	2					
	5		9	6				8
		3		8		9		
8				1	4		3	
					5	6		3
1							4	5
	6			3				

202

3		2			6			
			8		5		9	6
7						3	2	
		9	4		7	8		
	1	6						7
4	8		1		3			
			6			5		3

203

7		2		4		5		
	3							2
5		1	2				8	
2	6				8			
			4	5	6			
			1			6	8	
	1			7	8		4	
3						7		
		7		3		6		9

204

			7	6			3	
		8	4	2				6
3								
		2		3			9	4
4				8				3
6	7			5		8		
								2
5				4	2	6		
	9			7	6			

205

					1			4
	1	4	7		5	2		
	3					9	1	
				3				9
	7	9		8		6	5	
1				5				
	8	1					4	
		7	4		3	8	2	
5			6					

206

6			1	8				
						3	8	
	5	9	2				6	4
2	8							9
			5					
9							4	6
3	9			2		4	5	
	2	6						
			7	1				2

207

							8	7
	4	7	9					
8		1	6	7				
	8	5	3					
4								9
				6	2	1		
			5	7	1			6
			1	4	3			
9	1							

208

6			8					
	2		5					
	5		4	2		8	6	9
		1					9	3
			3		8			
2	4					7		
1	2	5		7	4		3	
				3		4		
				1				5

57

209

		9						
6	2	5	7			9	8	
	1							
	4		5		7			8
			8		4			
5			6		9		7	
							9	
	8	7			2	6	4	1
						2		

210

	1		4			8		9
7	9		6					
			5			6		
1		5			8			
8								6
			1			5		4
	5			2				
					5		4	1
2		8			7		9	

211

		7	6	2				
	9			4				
	2					7	1	
	7	6				3		
8			2					7
		2				5	6	
	6	4				5		
			1			2		
			8	9		6		

212

								8
1			2			7	3	
	2		7	8		1		
2	4	9						
		1	4		3	5		
						1	4	9
	8		2	3		6		
9	3			1				7
6								

58

	4		5		8			
9							6	5
	5				4	7		
					7			2
3			6	8	2			7
8			9					
		6	4				5	
2	3							4
			2		5		7	

		7	2	6	4		1	
								4
8		4			1		7	
1			9		8			
	9	2				1	8	
			1		7			3
	6		4			5		1
9								
	7		8	1	2	4		

				6		9		
		2		1				4
	1	8		2				5
5		9		6		2		
		3			4			
	2		3			8		6
9			1			3	6	
7			9		2			
		1		7				

		1						
		8				9	4	1
2	6			4				
	5			9		2	3	
				6				
	3	2		5			1	
			6				9	7
4	2	7				5		
				8				

		8						
	2	7	1		5			
4	9					1		7
	6			2				
8			6		3			2
			5			4		
3		1				9	4	
			8		2	3	1	
						8		

4			8		3		9	
	6					4		7
			4	6				
6		7				8	5	
		8				2		
	2	1				7		4
			3	8				
5		6					1	
	1		5		6			2

2	9		1			5		
4		7			2			
1								
			6		4		7	
3	4			8			6	5
	6		2		3			
								6
			3			7		9
		9			1		8	4

							7	
		4			7	8	9	
6			3	8				
8			4			7	2	
7								4
	4	1			2			5
			1	8				2
2	5	6				3		
	6							

221

2								
	6	3	1			8	5	
		7	8		3	4	2	
7			6	8				
				4	2			1
	7	1	5		8	2		
	8	2			7	6	1	
								9

222

	7						5	
	1				7			3
9			5	2				
		8	4	5				9
	9						6	
7				3	9	2		
				1	2			7
8			7				2	
	6						1	

223

6	5							3
7					2			
2	4	3			8			
4				9		3		
5				7				4
		8		5				2
			6			4	3	8
			1					5
3							2	6

224

	7		1					6
			5			8		4
				8			5	
7		1	6		3			
	2	7		5	4			
	8		3		6			7
	6			5				
1		4			7			
9				8		4		

4					5		2	
				6			5	7
	5			8	9			
		4	6				8	1
				9				
9	2				3	6		
			9	4			3	
7	1			2				
	4		3					6

				2		1		3
			9		1	2	8	
							5	7
5				4		7		
	8					1		
	9		6					4
6	3							
	2	8	3		5			
7		1		4				

2			7					4
		8			2		3	
			3	6	8			1
							8	3
		6		1		4		
1	4							
7		2	9	6				
	8		3			6		
3					7			2

3						4	1	
			6			9		5
			8	4			7	
8			4				9	
		4				5		
	9				7			8
	5			8	2			
7		3		1				
	2	9						4

					9		8	1
	1				3	5		
8		6			4	3	7	
4								3
	3						1	
9								5
	5	7	9			8		4
		8	4				2	
1	4		8					

		9		1	2			
		4			7		9	
		9				6		8
	1				3		5	
	9			7			4	
	8		1				3	
6		8			9			
	2		6			5		
			3	2		7		

	5						3	
8		1	4					2
			1		3			
	6	7						3
	4		2	3	6		5	
5						1	4	
			8		7			
3					2	7		8
	8						2	

	5		3				9	4
	7			2				
			1			3	5	
8	9				1			
1								9
		7					4	8
	8	2		6				
			3			2		
9	6				5		8	

233

1					5	7		
8	6	5						
		2	1				4	5
			3	9		7		
9				4				1
	2		5	6				
2	8				4	1		
						4	8	7
		7	8					9

234

			7		6		8	9
						4		
			9	8	3		6	2
	2		8	7			5	
	1			6	4		9	
5	4		6	1	8			
	1							
6	7		4		5			

235

		6	2					
	7	8			3		4	
	3				8			9
1		4		9				
			4	6	5			
				7		4		2
3			1				6	
	1		5			8	2	
					9	1		

236

	3		2			1		7
					7	2		
			6			9		3
5	1						4	7
			7		5			
9	7						5	2
2		8		5				
		9	8					
	5		3		2		8	

	4		7		6	2		
9								1
	7			1		8		
1			9		8			
	9					4		
		4	5					2
	6		2			7		
3								6
		9	4		5		2	

5								9
	4	3		5		6		
6				7				5
9	5			1	2			
	7						2	
			4	7			5	1
8			2					3
		7		6		5	9	
3								8

4		3			6	2	9	
						5	3	
				1				4
2				4				7
	8		2		3		4	
6				8				2
9				3				
	6	5						
	4	2	7			8		5

2		4		8				
			4				5	
7		8	6		1		9	
	1		9					6
3					8		2	
	4		8		2	9		1
	6			4				
			9			7		5

241

6		9		8			3	
		3			9		7	
1			3	2				
	4	6			5			
			9		6			
			7			3	6	
				7	4			6
	6		8			2		
	5			6		7		3

242

3		4						7
				3				
		1			6		5	3
				4		8	1	
6			1		5			4
	1	3		7				
5	4		7			2		
				6				
2						4		9

243

			2			6		
	4	9	8					
2	1	7				8		
5	3		7		8			
			1		3		7	8
		6				5	1	9
						7	3	6
		5			2			

244

3		9			1		8	
	1			2				
	5		7			6		
			4	8		1		
1	7						3	8
		4		1	3			
		3			2		6	
				7			9	
	8		9				3	2

					1			6
2	6	7						
		4				8		
1			6				2	
7		6		1		9		8
	8				7			3
		9				7		
						3	8	5
6			2					

2			6				8	
			3	1				7
	3			9			1	
	6		2			1	9	
			4					
	5	8			6		7	
	9			8			6	
5			7	6				
	8				3			5

				9	7		6	
					2	3		5
6							1	
	6							8
2		5		3		4		1
7						3		
	9							4
4		3	2					
	7		9	8				

	5	1						8
6				8	4			
3		8					5	
			6			3		5
			2	8	4			
7		6		9				
	3					6		4
		2	4					7
4						1	2	

249

			3	1		8	5	
						6	9	
		5		6		7		4
	7		2		4	1		
		3	6		5		2	
9		7		2		5		
	5	4						
	2	8		4	3			

250

						1		
			7	8			2	
1		7			2		4	
	1	2	6				7	
4				3				5
	9				5	6	8	
	4		5			7		3
	3			7	4			
		5						

251

8	2							
		9						8
			5		9			3
	3	8			4		6	
		4	2	1	6	3		
	1		8			2	9	
6			1		8			
3						5		
							7	2

252

					8			
	4		1			3		8
			8	9	5		1	
6	8	5					3	7
7	9					5	1	4
		1		6	2	8		
9		3			4		7	
			3					

9			7					
	7	2					4	
3			2	5				
		4		3	5		2	
		6			7			
	3		1	6		9		
			9	1				3
	8				5	7		
				6				9

			2				8	9
						5	1	
			7	3	1			
5				3	6			
2		7				9		8
		8	9					4
			3	8	4			
	5	2						
8	1				2			

		9		7				
3		8						5
	6			9	4		3	1
		1	3	8				
6								3
				2	9	1		
7	1		9	4			6	
8						9		7
				3		4		

	3		5		6		9	
5			3			7		
		4		2				3
						4	8	
				6				
	9	1						
3				4		8		
		6			5			7
	7			6		3		4

257

	4		6					7
	8				1	5	4	
		7	3			9		
3	6	2						
						2	7	5
		5			7	8		
	3	8	4				5	
6					8		2	

258

				3	5	1		
4			6			5		
3				8			7	
	6						2	
		4				6		
	5						9	
	4		3					8
	9				6			2
	3	7	9					

259

7				6	3	1		
					1	5	6	
		6		2	8			9
3	4	5						
						3	5	2
6				2	8		9	
	7	2	1					
		4	7	3				6

260

6	2			4	3			9
	3			7				
		8	1					3
	1		7					
2			6		5			4
					2		8	
5				9	3			
		5					7	
7			3	2			6	5

9							1			8	5
3					8	1		
			4			7		6
	8	2				6		
			8		6			
		3				2	5	
2		1		8				
		5	9					1
8	6		7					4

		5	1			9		3
	1			4	3			5
				8				7
		9						1
	3		6		4		5	
7						8		
3			2					
1			8	5			7	
6		7			9	5		

7			8		4	3		
	6	4	7				5	8
3					4			
		5	2					
	4	6				8	2	
				8	5			
		3						5
5	7				6	9	1	
		1	4		9			3

			3		4	7	8	
			6		8	5		
8							6	4
6			2	9			7	
9								6
	2			8	6			5
5	6							1
		1	8		2			
	9	2	1		5			

1				4		9		
			1		5			
2		4			8		5	1
8	7							
	5			9			2	
							8	6
6	2		5			3		7
			6		3			
		8		1				2

	2		9					
5	7	8			4			
				1			8	
		5			6			
7		6		8		2		1
		1				4		
	4			7				
		3				5	9	8
					1		4	

			7		1	5		
8								7
				8		3	9	1
					3	9	7	
			8		9			
	2	6	1					
2	6	5		3				
4								6
		7	6		5			

	4						3	9
1		3						
				5	2			
	7			8				5
	2		5	7	9		1	
6				3			9	
			7	9				
						8		4
7	8						2	

6	1						9	2
5			6	7	9			
	3							
			7			3	4	
			1		4			
	9	6			5			
							1	
			9	5	2			6
9	4						2	8

	4				9			
			8	4		3		
8		6		1				4
2	1							3
	5	8				9	1	
6							8	2
9				5		2		6
		4		6	1			
			2				5	

1

8	7	9	6	3	1	4	5	2
3	4	1	8	5	2	6	9	7
6	5	2	7	4	9	8	3	1
7	3	4	2	8	6	5	1	9
9	1	5	3	7	4	2	6	8
2	6	8	1	9	5	3	7	4
5	9	7	4	6	8	1	2	3
4	2	3	5	1	7	9	8	6
1	8	6	9	2	3	7	4	5

2

2	8	5	9	6	3	4	7	1
6	3	9	1	4	7	2	5	8
7	1	4	2	5	8	3	6	9
1	4	7	5	2	9	8	3	6
5	2	3	8	1	6	7	9	4
9	6	8	3	7	4	5	1	2
3	7	6	4	8	1	9	2	5
8	5	1	7	9	2	6	4	3
4	9	2	6	3	5	1	8	7

3

8	4	6	1	5	7	9	2	3
9	2	1	8	6	3	4	7	5
3	7	5	4	9	2	8	6	1
2	9	8	6	4	5	1	3	7
5	1	3	9	7	8	6	4	2
7	6	4	3	2	1	5	9	8
6	8	7	5	3	4	2	1	9
1	3	9	2	8	6	7	5	4
4	5	2	7	1	9	3	8	6

4

5	6	4	7	3	8	9	2	1
7	8	3	2	1	9	4	5	6
2	1	9	4	6	5	7	3	8
4	9	7	5	2	1	8	6	3
1	3	2	8	4	6	5	9	7
6	5	8	3	9	7	1	4	2
3	2	1	9	7	4	6	8	5
9	7	5	6	8	3	2	1	4
8	4	6	1	5	2	3	7	9

5

2	9	7	4	5	8	3	6	1
3	5	1	9	2	6	4	8	7
8	6	4	3	7	1	2	9	5
4	8	3	1	6	9	5	7	2
1	2	9	7	4	5	6	3	8
5	7	6	8	3	2	1	4	9
6	1	8	2	9	4	7	5	3
9	3	5	6	1	7	8	2	4
7	4	2	5	8	3	9	1	6

6

6	1	8	9	5	3	2	7	4
2	9	4	6	1	7	3	5	8
7	3	5	2	8	4	6	1	9
4	7	9	1	2	8	5	3	6
3	8	1	5	4	6	9	2	7
5	2	6	3	7	9	8	4	1
9	4	3	7	6	5	1	8	2
1	6	7	8	3	2	4	9	5
8	5	2	4	9	1	7	6	3

7

7	4	6	9	5	1	3	8	2
8	5	1	2	6	3	9	4	7
2	9	3	7	8	4	6	5	1
9	1	5	4	2	6	7	3	8
6	7	4	1	3	8	5	2	9
3	2	8	5	9	7	4	1	6
1	6	2	3	7	5	8	9	4
5	8	9	6	4	2	1	7	3
4	3	7	8	1	9	2	6	5

8

8	3	7	4	9	5	1	2	6
4	1	2	6	7	8	5	9	3
5	6	9	2	3	1	7	4	8
2	9	6	8	5	4	3	1	7
3	8	4	7	1	2	6	5	9
7	5	1	9	6	3	2	8	4
1	4	3	5	8	6	9	7	2
9	2	5	3	4	7	8	6	1
6	7	8	1	2	9	4	3	5

9

3	6	5	4	2	9	1	8	7
4	7	8	3	6	1	5	9	2
9	1	2	5	8	7	4	3	6
1	8	7	9	5	6	2	4	3
6	2	4	8	1	3	7	5	9
5	9	3	7	4	2	6	1	8
7	4	6	1	9	8	3	2	5
2	5	9	6	3	4	8	7	1
8	3	1	2	7	5	9	6	4

10

1	3	4	8	7	5	9	6	2
8	6	2	1	9	4	3	5	7
9	5	7	2	3	6	8	4	1
6	8	3	4	5	2	7	1	9
2	1	5	9	8	7	6	3	4
4	7	9	6	1	3	5	2	8
5	4	6	7	2	9	1	8	3
3	9	8	5	4	1	2	7	6
7	2	1	3	6	8	4	9	5

11

2	1	3	5	6	8	9	4	7
5	6	7	1	4	9	2	3	8
4	8	9	3	2	7	1	5	6
1	3	4	8	7	5	6	9	2
8	2	5	4	9	6	3	7	1
9	7	6	2	3	1	5	8	4
6	9	2	7	5	4	8	1	3
3	4	1	9	8	2	7	6	5
7	5	8	6	1	3	4	2	9

12

2	1	5	6	3	4	8	7	9
4	3	8	1	9	7	5	2	6
6	7	9	2	5	8	1	4	3
7	6	2	5	1	9	3	8	4
1	8	3	7	4	6	9	5	2
5	9	4	3	8	2	6	1	7
9	4	7	8	6	5	2	3	1
8	2	1	9	7	3	4	6	5
3	5	6	4	2	1	7	9	8

13

6	8	4	5	1	9	2	7	3
2	5	7	3	6	4	9	1	8
1	9	3	8	7	2	4	5	6
8	2	5	1	4	6	3	9	7
9	4	1	7	2	3	8	6	5
3	7	6	9	5	8	1	4	2
4	6	8	2	9	7	5	3	1
7	1	2	4	3	5	6	8	9
5	3	9	6	8	1	7	2	4

14

6	8	3	9	7	4	1	2	5
9	7	4	1	5	2	3	8	6
1	2	5	3	8	6	7	4	9
2	1	6	8	9	3	4	5	7
5	9	7	6	4	1	2	3	8
4	3	8	5	2	7	9	6	1
7	5	2	4	6	9	8	1	3
3	6	9	2	1	8	5	7	4
8	4	1	7	3	5	6	9	2

15

5	8	3	1	4	2	7	6	9
9	4	2	5	6	7	8	3	1
7	6	1	9	8	3	2	5	4
8	9	5	7	2	4	3	1	6
3	1	6	8	9	5	4	7	2
2	7	4	6	3	1	5	9	8
1	5	8	4	7	9	6	2	3
4	3	7	2	1	6	9	8	5
6	2	9	3	5	8	1	4	7

16

1	5	8	3	6	4	9	2	7
4	7	9	1	2	8	3	5	6
2	3	6	9	5	7	4	8	1
6	8	1	4	7	9	2	3	5
3	4	7	5	1	2	6	9	8
5	9	2	6	8	3	7	1	4
9	1	5	2	4	6	8	7	3
8	6	3	7	9	1	5	4	2
7	2	4	8	3	5	1	6	9

17

3	4	5	7	1	8	2	6	9
6	8	7	9	5	2	4	1	3
1	9	2	4	3	6	8	7	5
4	2	6	3	9	5	1	8	7
8	1	3	2	4	7	9	5	6
5	7	9	6	8	1	3	4	2
2	6	4	8	7	9	5	3	1
7	5	8	1	2	3	6	9	4
9	3	1	5	6	4	7	2	8

18

4	6	7	2	8	5	3	1	9
9	5	8	7	3	1	6	4	2
2	1	3	4	9	6	5	7	8
3	4	1	5	2	7	8	9	6
5	8	6	3	4	9	7	2	1
7	2	9	6	1	8	4	3	5
6	9	2	8	7	4	1	5	3
8	3	4	1	5	2	9	6	7
1	7	5	9	6	3	2	8	4

19

8	9	4	6	5	3	7	1	2
7	5	1	4	8	2	6	9	3
3	2	6	1	9	7	4	5	8
9	7	8	2	1	6	5	3	4
2	4	5	7	3	9	1	8	6
6	1	3	5	4	8	9	2	7
5	6	2	8	7	1	3	4	9
1	8	9	3	6	4	2	7	5
4	3	7	9	2	5	8	6	1

20

5	4	6	7	3	8	9	1	2
1	2	8	4	9	5	3	6	7
9	7	3	1	2	6	4	5	8
7	3	4	6	1	2	5	8	9
2	5	9	8	4	7	1	3	6
8	6	1	9	5	3	2	7	4
3	8	5	2	6	9	7	4	1
6	1	2	5	7	4	8	9	3
4	9	7	3	8	1	6	2	5

21

3	8	7	6	4	5	2	9	1
9	2	6	7	3	1	5	8	4
1	5	4	8	2	9	3	7	6
2	1	3	4	6	8	9	5	7
7	4	9	5	1	2	6	3	8
8	6	5	9	7	3	1	4	2
6	7	2	3	9	4	8	1	5
5	9	1	2	8	7	4	6	3
4	3	8	1	5	6	7	2	9

22

3	7	5	9	1	6	4	2	8
6	9	4	7	8	2	1	3	5
1	2	8	4	3	5	6	7	9
8	6	9	3	2	7	5	4	1
2	4	1	5	9	8	7	6	3
7	5	3	1	6	4	9	8	2
9	1	7	2	4	3	8	5	6
5	3	6	8	7	1	2	9	4
4	8	2	6	5	9	3	1	7

23

5	1	6	8	3	2	4	9	7
3	9	8	6	4	7	5	2	1
2	4	7	1	9	5	6	8	3
6	2	4	5	8	1	7	3	9
8	5	9	7	6	3	1	4	2
7	3	1	4	2	9	8	6	5
4	7	3	2	5	8	9	1	6
1	6	2	9	7	4	3	5	8
9	8	5	3	1	6	2	7	4

24

3	4	6	1	7	2	9	5	8
2	1	9	3	5	8	6	4	7
8	5	7	6	9	4	2	3	1
4	9	8	7	3	6	5	1	2
5	2	1	4	8	9	3	7	6
7	6	3	5	2	1	8	9	4
6	3	5	2	1	7	4	8	9
1	8	4	9	6	5	7	2	3
9	7	2	8	4	3	1	6	5

25

6	9	3	5	7	1	4	8	2
8	2	5	9	6	4	7	1	3
7	1	4	3	8	2	6	9	5
4	3	2	7	5	8	9	6	1
1	5	7	4	9	6	3	2	8
9	6	8	2	1	3	5	7	4
5	8	9	1	3	7	2	4	6
2	7	6	8	4	5	1	3	9
3	4	1	6	2	9	8	5	7

26

5	2	8	4	3	9	1	6	7
1	9	6	5	2	7	4	8	3
7	4	3	1	8	6	2	5	9
4	3	7	2	9	5	6	1	8
2	6	9	7	1	8	5	3	4
8	5	1	3	6	4	7	9	2
9	1	2	6	4	3	8	7	5
6	8	5	9	7	2	3	4	1
3	7	4	8	5	1	9	2	6

27

2	9	7	3	1	8	4	6	5
4	3	1	5	9	6	2	8	7
8	6	5	7	2	4	3	9	1
7	4	8	6	5	3	9	1	2
3	5	2	9	4	1	8	7	6
6	1	9	2	8	7	5	4	3
1	7	4	8	3	5	6	2	9
5	2	6	4	7	9	1	3	8
9	8	3	1	6	2	7	5	4

28

9	1	6	3	7	2	8	4	5
3	4	2	5	8	6	7	1	9
5	7	8	4	9	1	2	3	6
8	5	1	6	2	4	9	7	3
2	3	7	9	1	5	6	8	4
6	9	4	8	3	7	5	2	1
4	6	3	2	5	8	1	9	7
7	8	9	1	6	3	4	5	2
1	2	5	7	4	9	3	6	8

29

2	7	3	5	1	8	4	9	6
6	8	5	3	4	9	7	2	1
9	4	1	2	6	7	8	3	5
5	6	9	8	2	1	3	7	4
4	3	8	9	7	5	1	6	2
7	1	2	4	3	6	9	5	8
3	2	6	1	9	4	5	8	7
8	9	4	7	5	2	6	1	3
1	5	7	6	8	3	2	4	9

30

4	6	5	8	3	2	1	7	9
2	8	7	6	1	9	3	4	5
1	9	3	5	7	4	6	8	2
5	4	6	3	2	8	9	1	7
3	1	9	4	5	7	8	2	6
7	2	8	1	9	6	4	5	3
8	3	2	9	4	5	7	6	1
9	7	4	2	6	1	5	3	8
6	5	1	7	8	3	2	9	4

31

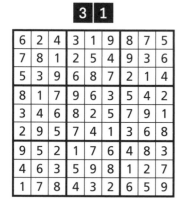

6	2	4	3	1	9	8	7	5
7	8	1	2	5	4	9	3	6
5	3	9	6	8	7	2	1	4
8	1	7	9	6	3	5	4	2
3	4	6	8	2	5	7	9	1
2	9	5	7	4	1	3	6	8
9	5	2	1	7	6	4	8	3
4	6	3	5	9	8	1	2	7
1	7	8	4	3	2	6	5	9

32

6	8	5	7	2	1	4	3	9
2	1	3	6	9	4	5	7	8
4	9	7	3	5	8	1	2	6
9	4	2	1	7	5	8	6	3
1	3	8	9	6	2	7	4	5
7	5	6	4	8	3	9	1	2
3	6	1	8	4	9	2	5	7
8	2	4	5	3	7	6	9	1
5	7	9	2	1	6	3	8	4

33

9	1	5	3	2	4	7	8	6
8	2	7	5	1	6	4	3	9
4	3	6	9	8	7	5	2	1
1	5	3	4	7	8	9	6	2
7	9	2	6	5	3	1	4	8
6	8	4	2	9	1	3	5	7
2	6	9	7	4	5	8	1	3
3	4	8	1	6	9	2	7	5
5	7	1	8	3	2	6	9	4

34

5	2	8	1	4	3	7	6	9
3	9	1	6	2	7	8	4	5
4	7	6	5	8	9	2	1	3
7	1	9	2	3	8	4	5	6
6	8	3	4	7	5	9	2	1
2	5	4	9	6	1	3	7	8
8	4	2	3	5	6	1	9	7
1	6	7	8	9	4	5	3	2
9	3	5	7	1	2	6	8	4

35

8	9	5	4	2	7	6	3	1
4	2	1	8	6	3	7	9	5
3	7	6	9	1	5	4	8	2
5	6	2	1	8	9	3	4	7
9	1	4	7	3	6	2	5	8
7	3	8	5	4	2	1	6	9
2	8	7	3	9	4	5	1	6
6	4	9	2	5	1	8	7	3
1	5	3	6	7	8	9	2	4

36

5	9	4	1	3	6	7	8	2
6	7	3	9	2	8	5	4	1
8	2	1	5	4	7	6	3	9
9	6	7	8	5	2	4	1	3
1	8	2	4	7	3	9	6	5
4	3	5	6	1	9	2	7	8
3	1	9	7	6	5	8	2	4
2	5	6	3	8	4	1	9	7
7	4	8	2	9	1	3	5	6

37

2	1	4	7	8	5	3	9	6
8	6	5	4	9	3	7	1	2
9	7	3	1	2	6	4	5	8
5	4	9	8	3	2	6	7	1
6	8	7	9	1	4	2	3	5
1	3	2	6	5	7	9	8	4
7	2	1	5	4	9	8	6	3
4	5	6	3	7	8	1	2	9
3	9	8	2	6	1	5	4	7

38

2	6	8	5	7	3	4	1	9
3	5	1	9	6	4	7	2	8
9	4	7	8	1	2	5	6	3
4	3	2	7	8	1	6	9	5
6	7	5	3	4	9	2	8	1
8	1	9	6	2	5	3	4	7
7	2	6	1	3	8	9	5	4
1	9	4	2	5	7	8	3	6
5	8	3	4	9	6	1	7	2

39

5	9	3	6	8	1	2	4	7
1	2	6	5	7	4	3	9	8
4	7	8	2	9	3	5	6	1
8	5	1	4	2	7	9	3	6
9	4	7	8	3	6	1	5	2
6	3	2	9	1	5	8	7	4
7	8	5	3	4	2	6	1	9
2	6	4	1	5	9	7	8	3
3	1	9	7	6	8	4	2	5

40

1	6	4	2	3	9	7	8	5
2	3	8	5	6	7	1	9	4
5	7	9	1	4	8	6	3	2
4	2	6	3	8	1	9	5	7
3	9	5	4	7	2	8	6	1
7	8	1	9	5	6	4	2	3
6	1	3	8	2	4	5	7	9
8	4	2	7	9	5	3	1	6
9	5	7	6	1	3	2	4	8

41

9	5	1	2	3	6	8	4	7
3	6	4	5	8	7	2	1	9
7	2	8	4	9	1	3	5	6
8	7	2	1	5	9	6	3	4
5	1	6	3	4	8	9	7	2
4	9	3	6	7	2	5	8	1
1	3	9	8	6	4	7	2	5
2	8	7	9	1	5	4	6	3
6	4	5	7	2	3	1	9	8

42

9	5	3	1	7	2	6	8	4
7	2	4	5	6	8	9	1	3
6	8	1	9	4	3	5	7	2
2	9	5	8	1	4	7	3	6
4	1	6	3	9	7	2	5	8
8	3	7	6	2	5	4	9	1
3	6	2	7	5	1	8	4	9
5	4	8	2	3	9	1	6	7
1	7	9	4	8	6	3	2	5

43

7	4	5	9	3	8	2	6	1
8	6	9	5	2	1	3	7	4
2	1	3	4	7	6	8	5	9
3	8	2	1	6	4	5	9	7
5	7	6	3	8	9	4	1	2
4	9	1	7	5	2	6	3	8
6	3	8	2	1	7	9	4	5
9	5	7	8	4	3	1	2	6
1	2	4	6	9	5	7	8	3

44

7	5	3	8	9	1	6	4	2
1	6	4	5	7	2	9	3	8
8	2	9	4	6	3	7	5	1
3	7	2	6	4	9	1	8	5
5	8	1	3	2	7	4	6	9
4	9	6	1	5	8	2	7	3
6	4	8	9	1	5	3	2	7
2	1	5	7	3	6	8	9	4
9	3	7	2	8	4	5	1	6

45

5	6	3	2	7	8	4	1	9
9	4	7	3	6	1	8	2	5
2	8	1	9	5	4	6	7	3
1	9	2	6	4	7	5	3	8
8	5	6	1	2	3	7	9	4
3	7	4	8	9	5	1	6	2
4	1	5	7	3	2	9	8	6
7	2	9	5	8	6	3	4	1
6	3	8	4	1	9	2	5	7

46

1	3	2	7	8	5	4	9	6
5	6	9	4	3	1	7	2	8
7	8	4	6	9	2	3	5	1
2	9	6	5	4	8	1	7	3
4	1	5	2	7	3	8	6	9
3	7	8	1	6	9	5	4	2
9	4	7	8	1	6	2	3	5
6	2	1	3	5	4	9	8	7
8	5	3	9	2	7	6	1	4

47

8	6	1	9	2	5	7	3	4
9	7	5	6	4	3	8	2	1
3	4	2	8	7	1	6	5	9
6	2	4	3	9	7	1	8	5
1	9	8	5	6	4	2	7	3
5	3	7	1	8	2	4	9	6
4	1	3	2	5	8	9	6	7
7	8	9	4	3	6	5	1	2
2	5	6	7	1	9	3	4	8

48

5	4	9	8	6	3	2	1	7
6	1	7	5	9	2	3	8	4
8	2	3	1	7	4	5	6	9
7	9	6	4	8	5	1	2	3
2	3	5	6	1	7	4	9	8
4	8	1	2	3	9	7	5	6
3	5	2	9	4	8	6	7	1
1	7	8	3	2	6	9	4	5
9	6	4	7	5	1	8	3	2

49

3	1	5	9	4	8	6	7	2
7	9	4	5	2	6	1	8	3
6	2	8	3	7	1	5	4	9
1	4	7	8	9	3	2	6	5
2	5	3	7	6	4	8	9	1
9	8	6	2	1	5	4	3	7
8	7	2	6	5	9	3	1	4
4	6	9	1	3	2	7	5	8
5	3	1	4	8	7	9	2	6

50

8	5	9	2	6	3	7	4	1
4	2	1	9	7	5	8	6	3
3	7	6	1	4	8	2	9	5
5	8	7	6	2	4	1	3	9
6	1	3	5	8	9	4	2	7
9	4	2	7	3	1	5	8	6
1	9	8	3	5	2	6	7	4
2	6	5	4	9	7	3	1	8
7	3	4	8	1	6	9	5	2

51

5	1	8	6	3	7	4	9	2
4	3	6	2	9	8	1	5	7
7	9	2	4	1	5	6	8	3
6	7	5	8	2	9	3	1	4
8	4	1	5	7	3	9	2	6
9	2	3	1	4	6	8	7	5
2	6	7	3	8	1	5	4	9
3	8	9	7	5	4	2	6	1
1	5	4	9	6	2	7	3	8

52

4	1	9	2	5	6	8	3	7
5	6	3	4	8	7	9	2	1
8	7	2	9	1	3	5	6	4
1	3	7	6	9	8	2	4	5
6	9	5	3	2	4	7	1	8
2	8	4	1	7	5	3	9	6
9	5	1	8	6	2	4	7	3
3	2	8	7	4	1	6	5	9
7	4	6	5	3	9	1	8	2

53

7	4	6	8	2	1	5	9	3
5	9	2	3	7	6	1	4	8
1	8	3	5	9	4	6	2	7
9	6	7	1	4	5	3	8	2
2	3	1	9	6	8	4	7	5
4	5	8	7	3	2	9	1	6
3	2	4	6	1	7	8	5	9
6	7	5	4	8	9	2	3	1
8	1	9	2	5	3	7	6	4

54

8	6	1	2	3	7	5	4	9
3	2	4	8	9	5	1	6	7
7	5	9	6	1	4	2	3	8
1	4	5	9	2	3	8	7	6
2	7	6	4	8	1	9	5	3
9	8	3	5	7	6	4	1	2
6	3	2	1	4	8	7	9	5
5	1	8	7	6	9	3	2	4
4	9	7	3	5	2	6	8	1

55

8	3	5	1	9	7	6	2	4
6	7	9	5	4	2	8	1	3
2	4	1	8	3	6	9	5	7
4	5	8	3	7	1	2	9	6
9	1	6	2	8	4	3	7	5
7	2	3	6	5	9	4	8	1
1	6	4	9	2	5	7	3	8
5	8	2	7	6	3	1	4	9
3	9	7	4	1	8	5	6	2

56

1	3	4	5	6	9	8	7	2
8	2	5	4	1	7	9	3	6
9	6	7	8	2	3	5	1	4
7	5	8	9	4	2	1	6	3
3	4	6	7	8	1	2	9	5
2	1	9	3	5	6	4	8	7
5	8	3	6	9	4	7	2	1
6	9	2	1	7	5	3	4	8
4	7	1	2	3	8	6	5	9

57

1	2	7	8	5	9	3	6	4
9	6	5	1	3	4	8	2	7
4	8	3	7	2	6	1	9	5
8	9	4	5	6	1	2	7	3
6	7	2	4	8	3	9	5	1
5	3	1	9	7	2	6	4	8
2	5	6	3	4	8	7	1	9
3	4	9	2	1	7	5	8	6
7	1	8	6	9	5	4	3	2

58

9	3	7	4	6	2	8	5	1
6	8	4	7	5	1	2	9	3
5	1	2	3	9	8	6	7	4
3	7	8	1	4	5	9	6	2
2	6	5	8	3	9	1	4	7
4	9	1	2	7	6	3	8	5
7	5	9	6	2	3	4	1	8
8	2	6	5	1	4	7	3	9
1	4	3	9	8	7	5	2	6

59

4	5	8	7	1	2	6	3	9
2	3	6	8	9	5	1	4	7
1	9	7	3	6	4	8	2	5
8	1	9	5	7	3	2	6	4
5	6	4	9	2	8	7	1	3
7	2	3	1	4	6	5	9	8
9	8	2	4	5	1	3	7	6
6	4	5	2	3	7	9	8	1
3	7	1	6	8	9	4	5	2

60

8	6	4	1	5	7	9	3	2
7	5	1	3	9	2	8	4	6
9	2	3	8	4	6	5	7	1
2	4	8	6	7	3	1	5	9
3	7	9	5	8	1	2	6	4
5	1	6	4	2	9	3	8	7
4	9	2	7	3	8	6	1	5
1	3	7	2	6	5	4	9	8
6	8	5	9	1	4	7	2	3

6 1

8	2	7	9	3	4	5	1	6
1	4	6	2	7	5	3	8	9
9	5	3	1	8	6	4	7	2
6	9	2	4	1	8	7	3	5
5	3	8	6	9	7	1	2	4
4	7	1	3	5	2	9	6	8
3	1	5	8	2	9	6	4	7
7	8	4	5	6	3	2	9	1
2	6	9	7	4	1	8	5	3

6 2

8	6	1	3	2	5	4	9	7
4	7	9	1	8	6	5	3	2
5	3	2	4	7	9	8	1	6
1	4	7	2	6	8	9	5	3
9	8	3	7	5	1	2	6	4
6	2	5	9	3	4	1	7	8
7	9	8	6	1	2	3	4	5
2	1	6	5	4	3	7	8	9
3	5	4	8	9	7	6	2	1

6 3

2	4	9	6	1	7	8	3	5
1	7	6	3	8	5	2	4	9
5	8	3	9	2	4	6	7	1
4	5	7	8	6	9	3	1	2
3	1	8	7	5	2	9	6	4
6	9	2	4	3	1	7	5	8
8	3	5	2	4	6	1	9	7
7	2	1	5	9	3	4	8	6
9	6	4	1	7	8	5	2	3

6 4

5	6	7	3	8	4	9	2	1
9	8	3	2	5	1	6	7	4
1	4	2	6	7	9	8	5	3
3	7	9	1	6	5	4	8	2
4	1	8	7	2	3	5	9	6
6	2	5	9	4	8	3	1	7
2	3	4	5	9	7	1	6	8
8	9	6	4	1	2	7	3	5
7	5	1	8	3	6	2	4	9

6 5

7	1	8	3	2	9	4	6	5
9	2	4	7	6	5	1	8	3
3	6	5	1	8	4	9	2	7
2	4	7	9	5	1	6	3	8
5	8	3	2	4	6	7	9	1
1	9	6	8	7	3	2	5	4
4	3	1	6	9	8	5	7	2
6	5	2	4	3	7	8	1	9
8	7	9	5	1	2	3	4	6

6 6

2	3	8	5	6	4	7	1	9
4	1	9	8	2	7	6	5	3
7	6	5	1	3	9	8	2	4
3	9	6	7	1	8	5	4	2
5	8	7	9	4	2	1	3	6
1	2	4	3	5	6	9	7	8
6	5	3	4	8	1	2	9	7
8	7	1	2	9	3	4	6	5
9	4	2	6	7	5	3	8	1

6 7

4	7	8	9	2	6	1	5	3
2	6	3	5	7	1	8	9	4
5	9	1	8	4	3	7	2	6
9	8	6	2	5	7	4	3	1
1	3	2	4	6	8	9	7	5
7	4	5	1	3	9	2	6	8
3	5	4	7	8	2	6	1	9
6	2	9	3	1	4	5	8	7
8	1	7	6	9	5	3	4	2

6 8

1	8	6	3	5	7	4	2	9
7	3	5	4	9	2	6	8	1
4	2	9	8	1	6	3	7	5
8	4	7	9	6	1	2	5	3
3	5	1	7	2	8	9	4	6
9	6	2	5	4	3	7	1	8
6	1	4	2	8	9	5	3	7
5	9	3	1	7	4	8	6	2
2	7	8	6	3	5	1	9	4

6 9

5	1	6	2	4	8	3	9	7
7	8	3	6	1	9	5	2	4
4	9	2	7	5	3	6	1	8
6	2	1	4	9	7	8	3	5
8	7	4	3	2	5	9	6	1
3	5	9	1	8	6	7	4	2
9	4	5	8	6	1	2	7	3
1	6	7	5	3	2	4	8	9
2	3	8	9	7	4	1	5	6

7 0

9	2	4	7	1	5	8	3	6
7	8	5	9	6	3	2	1	4
6	3	1	4	8	2	7	9	5
2	1	9	3	7	4	6	5	8
4	6	8	1	5	9	3	2	7
5	7	3	6	2	8	9	4	1
1	9	2	8	4	7	5	6	3
8	5	6	2	3	1	4	7	9
3	4	7	5	9	6	1	8	2

7 1

2	3	8	7	5	9	6	4	1
4	7	9	3	6	1	5	2	8
5	6	1	4	2	8	9	3	7
9	2	5	6	8	7	3	1	4
3	4	6	5	1	2	8	7	9
1	8	7	9	4	3	2	5	6
8	5	3	1	7	6	4	9	2
6	1	4	2	9	5	7	8	3
7	9	2	8	3	4	1	6	5

7 2

1	3	5	7	4	2	6	8	9
2	6	8	9	1	3	7	5	4
4	9	7	5	6	8	1	3	2
8	7	3	4	2	6	9	1	5
6	4	9	3	5	1	8	2	7
5	2	1	8	9	7	3	4	6
7	5	2	1	3	9	4	6	8
3	8	4	6	7	5	2	9	1
9	1	6	2	8	4	5	7	3

73

1	2	8	4	3	9	6	5	7
6	3	5	1	8	7	9	2	4
9	7	4	5	6	2	8	3	1
4	8	7	3	1	5	2	6	9
5	1	9	7	2	6	3	4	8
2	6	3	8	9	4	1	7	5
7	9	6	2	5	1	4	8	3
3	5	1	6	4	8	7	9	2
8	4	2	9	7	3	5	1	6

74

9	2	1	5	4	3	7	6	8
7	6	8	2	1	9	5	4	3
3	5	4	8	7	6	9	1	2
2	9	3	1	5	4	8	7	6
6	4	5	9	8	7	2	3	1
8	1	7	6	3	2	4	9	5
1	3	2	7	9	5	6	8	4
4	7	6	3	2	8	1	5	9
5	8	9	4	6	1	3	2	7

75

4	2	8	7	9	5	3	6	1
7	1	6	8	3	2	9	5	4
5	9	3	4	6	1	7	8	2
1	4	7	9	5	3	8	2	6
6	8	9	2	7	4	1	3	5
3	5	2	1	8	6	4	7	9
9	3	1	5	2	7	6	4	8
2	6	4	3	1	8	5	9	7
8	7	5	6	4	9	2	1	3

76

5	9	7	1	6	4	2	3	8
6	3	2	9	7	8	5	1	4
8	4	1	3	2	5	9	7	6
9	1	3	6	8	7	4	5	2
2	8	6	5	4	1	3	9	7
4	7	5	2	9	3	6	8	1
3	6	9	8	1	2	7	4	5
1	5	4	7	3	6	8	2	9
7	2	8	4	5	9	1	6	3

77

2	3	6	5	8	7	9	1	4
8	7	4	3	1	9	6	5	2
9	5	1	6	4	2	8	7	3
3	8	5	4	2	6	1	9	7
7	1	9	8	5	3	4	2	6
4	6	2	7	9	1	3	8	5
1	2	7	9	6	4	5	3	8
6	9	8	2	3	5	7	4	1
5	4	3	1	7	8	2	6	9

78

2	1	8	6	4	9	5	7	3
5	6	4	3	7	1	8	9	2
9	7	3	2	5	8	6	1	4
3	4	9	7	6	2	1	5	8
7	5	6	1	8	3	4	2	9
1	8	2	5	9	4	7	3	6
4	2	5	8	3	7	9	6	1
8	3	7	9	1	6	2	4	5
6	9	1	4	2	5	3	8	7

79

6	9	2	4	3	1	7	5	8
7	4	8	6	9	5	3	1	2
5	3	1	2	8	7	6	4	9
8	6	7	5	1	4	2	9	3
1	5	3	9	2	6	4	8	7
9	2	4	3	7	8	1	6	5
4	7	5	8	6	2	9	3	1
2	8	9	1	4	3	5	7	6
3	1	6	7	5	9	8	2	4

80

9	7	6	3	1	8	4	5	2
1	5	2	7	4	6	3	9	8
3	8	4	2	5	9	6	1	7
4	6	9	8	7	2	5	3	1
8	3	7	5	6	1	2	4	9
5	2	1	9	3	4	8	7	6
2	9	3	1	8	5	7	6	4
7	4	8	6	9	3	1	2	5
6	1	5	4	2	7	9	8	3

81

2	4	9	8	7	5	6	3	1
7	1	3	4	6	2	8	9	5
6	8	5	1	9	3	2	4	7
1	3	4	7	8	9	5	2	6
9	5	2	3	1	6	7	8	4
8	6	7	5	2	4	9	1	3
4	7	6	2	3	8	1	5	9
3	2	1	9	5	7	4	6	8
5	9	8	6	4	1	3	7	2

82

2	6	3	7	5	9	4	8	1
8	9	7	1	6	4	2	5	3
4	5	1	2	8	3	6	7	9
3	4	2	5	9	8	1	6	7
7	1	6	4	3	2	5	9	8
5	8	9	6	1	7	3	4	2
1	7	8	3	4	5	9	2	6
6	2	4	9	7	1	8	3	5
9	3	5	8	2	6	7	1	4

83

8	9	1	5	2	6	7	3	4
4	5	7	8	1	3	2	6	9
2	6	3	4	7	9	8	5	1
3	2	4	1	6	7	5	9	8
1	7	5	9	8	2	3	4	6
6	8	9	3	5	4	1	7	2
7	1	8	6	9	5	4	2	3
9	3	2	7	4	1	6	8	5
5	4	6	2	3	8	9	1	7

84

3	9	4	7	2	5	6	8	1
7	5	2	6	1	8	4	9	3
8	1	6	4	3	9	2	7	5
1	7	9	2	5	4	8	3	6
2	4	8	9	6	3	1	5	7
6	3	5	1	8	7	9	2	4
5	6	1	8	7	2	3	4	9
9	8	3	5	4	6	7	1	2
4	2	7	3	9	1	5	6	8

85

4	1	9	5	6	7	3	8	2
6	8	5	9	3	2	4	7	1
3	7	2	8	4	1	6	9	5
8	4	6	3	2	9	5	1	7
5	9	7	1	8	6	2	3	4
2	3	1	7	5	4	8	6	9
9	2	3	4	1	8	7	5	6
1	5	4	6	7	3	9	2	8
7	6	8	2	9	5	1	4	3

86

4	7	1	8	9	5	2	6	3
8	6	9	1	2	3	7	5	4
3	2	5	7	6	4	1	9	8
6	1	3	2	4	8	9	7	5
9	5	4	6	3	7	8	2	1
7	8	2	5	1	9	3	4	6
2	3	6	9	5	1	4	8	7
1	9	7	4	8	6	5	3	2
5	4	8	3	7	2	6	1	9

87

4	1	7	2	3	6	5	8	9
6	2	8	4	5	9	7	3	1
3	9	5	7	8	1	4	2	6
7	3	9	5	6	4	2	1	8
2	5	6	8	1	7	3	9	4
1	8	4	3	9	2	6	5	7
8	6	3	9	4	5	1	7	2
9	7	1	6	2	3	8	4	5
5	4	2	1	7	8	9	6	3

88

2	5	7	3	9	4	6	1	8
8	4	6	1	2	7	3	9	5
3	1	9	6	8	5	4	2	7
7	9	8	2	1	6	5	4	3
4	2	3	7	5	8	9	6	1
5	6	1	9	4	3	7	8	2
1	8	4	5	3	9	2	7	6
9	7	5	8	6	2	1	3	4
6	3	2	4	7	1	8	5	9

89

1	2	3	6	7	9	5	8	4
9	8	6	5	3	4	7	1	2
4	5	7	8	1	2	9	6	3
3	9	5	4	8	6	1	2	7
2	1	8	7	9	5	4	3	6
7	6	4	1	2	3	8	5	9
8	4	9	3	6	1	2	7	5
6	7	2	9	5	8	3	4	1
5	3	1	2	4	7	6	9	8

90

3	5	9	7	4	6	2	8	1
6	8	1	5	2	3	9	7	4
4	2	7	1	8	9	6	3	5
5	6	8	2	3	7	4	1	9
9	1	4	8	6	5	7	2	3
2	7	3	9	1	4	8	5	6
1	4	5	6	7	2	3	9	8
8	3	2	4	9	1	5	6	7
7	9	6	3	5	8	1	4	2

91

5	9	7	1	8	4	6	3	2
2	6	1	5	3	9	7	8	4
8	4	3	2	7	6	1	9	5
1	5	6	3	9	7	2	4	8
4	2	9	6	5	8	3	1	7
7	3	8	4	2	1	9	5	6
3	7	2	8	1	5	4	6	9
6	1	5	9	4	2	8	7	3
9	8	4	7	6	3	5	2	1

92

8	7	2	3	1	5	9	6	4
5	6	1	9	7	4	8	2	3
9	3	4	8	6	2	7	5	1
4	5	3	6	9	1	2	8	7
1	2	6	4	8	7	3	9	5
7	9	8	2	5	3	4	1	6
2	1	9	7	4	6	5	3	8
6	8	7	5	3	9	1	4	2
3	4	5	1	2	8	6	7	9

93

6	9	8	3	4	1	2	7	5
4	1	3	7	2	5	9	8	6
7	5	2	8	6	9	4	3	1
1	2	7	9	8	6	5	4	3
5	3	4	2	1	7	6	9	8
9	8	6	5	3	4	7	1	2
3	4	5	1	9	2	8	6	7
8	7	9	6	5	3	1	2	4
2	6	1	4	7	8	3	5	9

94

8	7	1	9	5	4	3	6	2
3	2	6	1	8	7	9	5	4
9	5	4	2	3	6	7	8	1
6	9	5	3	4	8	2	1	7
1	8	7	5	2	9	4	3	6
4	3	2	6	7	1	5	9	8
2	4	9	8	1	5	6	7	3
7	6	8	4	9	3	1	2	5
5	1	3	7	6	2	8	4	9

95

2	3	5	8	7	1	4	9	6
1	6	9	2	5	4	8	7	3
7	4	8	6	3	9	1	5	2
3	7	2	4	1	6	5	8	9
9	8	4	3	2	5	7	6	1
6	5	1	9	8	7	3	2	4
4	2	3	7	6	8	9	1	5
5	9	7	1	4	2	6	3	8
8	1	6	5	9	3	2	4	7

96

9	3	5	7	1	8	6	4	2
1	8	2	5	4	6	3	7	9
7	4	6	9	3	2	1	8	5
4	1	3	2	6	7	5	9	8
8	5	7	3	9	1	4	2	6
2	6	9	4	8	5	7	3	1
3	2	8	1	5	4	9	6	7
6	9	1	8	7	3	2	5	4
5	7	4	6	2	9	8	1	3

97

6	7	4	9	3	5	1	8	2
3	1	9	8	4	2	6	7	5
8	5	2	7	1	6	4	9	3
7	4	6	1	2	8	5	3	9
2	3	5	4	9	7	8	1	6
1	9	8	5	6	3	7	2	4
4	6	1	2	7	9	3	5	8
5	2	7	3	8	4	9	6	1
9	8	3	6	5	1	2	4	7

98

5	3	7	2	6	9	1	8	4
1	4	6	8	7	3	5	2	9
8	9	2	4	1	5	6	3	7
6	2	4	1	3	7	8	9	5
9	8	3	6	5	2	7	4	1
7	5	1	9	8	4	3	6	2
2	1	8	5	4	6	9	7	3
3	6	9	7	2	1	4	5	8
4	7	5	3	9	8	2	1	6

99

3	4	5	9	2	7	1	6	8
1	6	8	4	5	3	2	9	7
9	7	2	8	1	6	4	5	3
5	8	1	6	3	4	7	2	9
6	3	9	7	8	2	5	1	4
4	2	7	5	9	1	3	8	6
8	5	3	2	4	9	6	7	1
2	1	6	3	7	8	9	4	5
7	9	4	1	6	5	8	3	2

100

5	2	6	9	3	7	8	4	1
8	4	7	5	2	1	9	6	3
9	1	3	4	8	6	5	7	2
7	3	5	8	6	4	1	2	9
4	8	9	3	1	2	6	5	7
2	6	1	7	5	9	3	8	4
3	9	2	6	7	8	4	1	5
1	5	8	2	4	3	7	9	6
6	7	4	1	9	5	2	3	8

101

3	4	8	5	7	9	6	2	1
7	9	6	4	2	1	3	5	8
1	5	2	3	6	8	4	9	7
9	1	5	6	3	7	2	8	4
2	3	7	9	8	4	1	6	5
8	6	4	1	5	2	7	3	9
6	8	1	2	4	5	9	7	3
4	7	3	8	9	6	5	1	2
5	2	9	7	1	3	8	4	6

102

4	7	1	2	8	5	9	3	6
8	2	6	1	3	9	7	5	4
9	5	3	7	4	6	8	2	1
1	4	7	3	2	8	5	6	9
5	6	2	9	7	1	3	4	8
3	8	9	6	5	4	1	7	2
2	3	8	4	9	7	6	1	5
7	1	5	8	6	2	4	9	3
6	9	4	5	1	3	2	8	7

103

7	5	8	9	1	4	3	2	6
2	1	4	8	3	6	7	5	9
9	3	6	5	7	2	4	8	1
1	7	3	6	9	8	5	4	2
5	4	9	3	2	1	8	6	7
6	8	2	7	4	5	9	1	3
3	6	5	1	8	9	2	7	4
8	2	7	4	6	3	1	9	5
4	9	1	2	5	7	6	3	8

104

9	1	2	4	8	3	7	6	5
4	8	3	5	6	7	2	9	1
5	6	7	2	1	9	8	3	4
7	9	6	1	3	2	5	4	8
1	5	8	7	9	4	3	2	6
3	2	4	8	5	6	1	7	9
8	7	9	3	4	1	6	5	2
2	4	1	6	7	5	9	8	3
6	3	5	9	2	8	4	1	7

105

6	1	7	4	3	5	2	9	8
4	8	5	1	9	2	7	3	6
2	9	3	7	8	6	5	4	1
5	7	2	6	4	3	8	1	9
3	6	9	2	1	8	4	5	7
8	4	1	9	5	7	6	2	3
7	2	4	3	6	9	1	8	5
1	3	8	5	7	4	9	6	2
9	5	6	8	2	1	3	7	4

106

4	8	6	7	2	9	1	3	5
1	2	5	3	8	6	7	9	4
7	3	9	5	1	4	2	6	8
2	9	1	6	7	5	4	8	3
3	6	8	4	9	1	5	2	7
5	7	4	2	3	8	9	1	6
8	5	2	1	6	7	3	4	9
9	1	7	8	4	3	6	5	2
6	4	3	9	5	2	8	7	1

107

6	5	4	2	8	1	9	7	3
9	3	7	5	4	6	2	1	8
8	1	2	9	3	7	6	5	4
1	8	3	4	2	5	7	6	9
2	7	9	6	1	3	4	8	5
5	4	6	8	7	9	1	3	2
3	2	5	7	6	4	8	9	1
7	9	8	1	5	2	3	4	6
4	6	1	3	9	8	5	2	7

108

8	9	1	3	6	7	2	4	5
6	7	2	8	5	4	3	9	1
5	3	4	1	2	9	6	7	8
4	1	7	2	8	5	9	3	6
3	5	9	6	4	1	8	2	7
2	6	8	7	9	3	1	5	4
9	4	6	5	1	2	7	8	3
1	2	3	4	7	8	5	6	9
7	8	5	9	3	6	4	1	2

109

7	2	8	6	1	9	4	5	3
3	6	9	2	5	4	7	8	1
4	1	5	3	8	7	2	9	6
8	9	1	5	4	6	3	2	7
5	3	6	7	2	8	1	4	9
2	7	4	1	9	3	8	6	5
9	8	7	4	6	1	5	3	2
6	5	3	8	7	2	9	1	4
1	4	2	9	3	5	6	7	8

110

8	1	7	2	6	5	3	4	9
2	4	9	3	1	7	6	5	8
6	3	5	4	9	8	2	7	1
9	7	4	6	2	3	1	8	5
1	6	3	5	8	9	7	2	4
5	2	8	7	4	1	9	3	6
3	8	2	9	5	6	4	1	7
4	5	6	1	7	2	8	9	3
7	9	1	8	3	4	5	6	2

111

4	9	1	8	2	3	6	5	7
3	7	5	1	9	6	4	2	8
6	2	8	5	7	4	9	3	1
2	6	7	4	3	9	8	1	5
5	3	4	6	1	8	2	7	9
1	8	9	7	5	2	3	6	4
7	4	6	3	8	1	5	9	2
8	5	2	9	6	7	1	4	3
9	1	3	2	4	5	7	8	6

112

1	3	2	6	7	9	5	8	4
9	7	5	8	1	4	6	2	3
4	6	8	5	2	3	9	1	7
2	4	7	3	6	1	8	9	5
3	8	9	4	5	2	1	7	6
5	1	6	9	8	7	3	4	2
7	9	4	1	3	6	2	5	8
6	5	1	2	4	8	7	3	9
8	2	3	7	9	5	4	6	1

113

9	2	4	1	5	7	3	6	8
8	6	5	3	2	4	9	1	7
1	3	7	8	6	9	5	4	2
3	9	8	6	4	5	7	2	1
6	5	2	7	9	1	8	3	4
4	7	1	2	3	8	6	5	9
5	4	6	9	7	2	1	8	3
2	8	9	5	1	3	4	7	6
7	1	3	4	8	6	2	9	5

114

8	7	4	1	5	6	3	2	9
3	6	9	2	4	8	1	5	7
5	2	1	7	3	9	4	6	8
9	5	6	4	1	7	8	3	2
2	3	7	6	8	5	9	4	1
4	1	8	9	2	3	6	7	5
1	4	3	5	9	2	7	8	6
7	8	2	3	6	1	5	9	4
6	9	5	8	7	4	2	1	3

115

1	4	5	8	9	7	6	3	2
2	3	9	1	4	6	5	8	7
6	8	7	2	5	3	4	1	9
3	2	8	6	1	5	9	7	4
7	5	1	9	2	4	3	6	8
9	6	4	7	3	8	1	2	5
8	1	6	4	7	9	2	5	3
4	7	3	5	6	2	8	9	1
5	9	2	3	8	1	7	4	6

116

7	4	3	5	6	9	8	2	1
1	8	2	3	7	4	6	5	9
6	9	5	1	8	2	7	4	3
3	2	6	7	5	8	1	9	4
4	1	7	9	2	6	5	3	8
8	5	9	4	1	3	2	7	6
5	6	4	8	3	7	9	1	2
2	3	1	6	9	5	4	8	7
9	7	8	2	4	1	3	6	5

117

4	5	7	1	8	6	9	3	2
2	8	6	3	7	9	5	1	4
1	3	9	4	2	5	8	7	6
3	9	1	5	4	2	7	6	8
6	2	5	7	3	8	1	4	9
7	4	8	6	9	1	2	5	3
9	7	3	2	5	4	6	8	1
8	1	4	9	6	7	3	2	5
5	6	2	8	1	3	4	9	7

118

9	5	6	1	8	4	3	2	7
3	4	8	2	7	6	5	1	9
2	7	1	9	3	5	4	6	8
5	3	4	8	6	9	1	7	2
8	1	9	7	2	3	6	5	4
7	6	2	5	4	1	9	8	3
6	8	3	4	5	7	2	9	1
4	9	7	6	1	2	8	3	5
1	2	5	3	9	8	7	4	6

119

5	2	8	9	3	1	6	7	4
3	4	6	5	7	8	1	2	9
7	9	1	4	2	6	8	5	3
9	5	3	2	8	4	7	6	1
2	8	7	1	6	9	3	4	5
1	6	4	7	5	3	9	8	2
8	7	9	3	4	2	5	1	6
6	3	2	8	1	5	4	9	7
4	1	5	6	9	7	2	3	8

120

5	2	8	7	6	3	4	9	1
6	7	3	1	9	4	8	5	2
4	9	1	8	5	2	7	3	6
1	6	5	3	2	8	9	7	4
8	3	7	4	1	9	2	6	5
9	4	2	5	7	6	3	1	8
3	1	9	2	4	5	6	8	7
2	5	6	9	8	7	1	4	3
7	8	4	6	3	1	5	2	9

1 2 1

9	4	8	2	3	1	6	5	7
5	3	7	4	9	6	2	8	1
1	2	6	5	8	7	4	9	3
3	9	4	6	1	2	5	7	8
7	6	5	8	4	3	9	1	2
8	1	2	7	5	9	3	4	6
4	8	1	3	6	5	7	2	9
6	7	9	1	2	4	8	3	5
2	5	3	9	7	8	1	6	4

1 2 2

4	5	7	9	3	2	8	6	1
8	1	2	5	7	6	3	4	9
3	6	9	8	1	4	5	7	2
9	8	1	2	5	7	6	3	4
5	4	6	3	9	8	1	2	7
7	2	3	4	6	1	9	5	8
2	3	4	1	8	5	7	9	6
1	7	5	6	4	9	2	8	3
6	9	8	7	2	3	4	1	5

1 2 3

6	9	7	1	8	2	3	5	4
3	2	5	7	4	9	8	6	1
1	8	4	5	6	3	9	2	7
8	5	9	6	3	7	1	4	2
7	3	1	4	2	8	5	9	6
4	6	2	9	1	5	7	8	3
5	7	6	2	9	1	4	3	8
9	4	8	3	7	6	2	1	5
2	1	3	8	5	4	6	7	9

1 2 4

3	9	4	1	2	7	5	6	8
5	6	2	9	4	8	3	1	7
7	1	8	6	3	5	9	4	2
4	5	6	8	9	1	2	7	3
1	2	3	5	7	4	6	8	9
9	8	7	3	6	2	4	5	1
6	7	5	2	1	9	8	3	4
2	3	1	4	8	6	7	9	5
8	4	9	7	5	3	1	2	6

1 2 5

7	2	6	9	1	3	8	4	5
9	1	3	8	4	5	2	6	7
5	8	4	6	2	7	9	3	1
3	9	1	4	8	2	7	5	6
8	7	2	3	5	6	4	1	9
4	6	5	1	7	9	3	8	2
6	3	7	5	9	4	1	2	8
2	5	8	7	3	1	6	9	4
1	4	9	2	6	8	5	7	3

1 2 6

6	4	7	1	3	9	8	5	2
2	8	5	4	6	7	3	1	9
1	3	9	5	2	8	4	7	6
5	1	2	3	4	6	9	8	7
7	9	4	2	8	1	6	3	5
3	6	8	7	9	5	1	2	4
9	2	3	8	7	4	5	6	1
4	7	1	6	5	3	2	9	8
8	5	6	9	1	2	7	4	3

1 2 7

3	9	4	5	2	6	1	8	7
7	1	6	4	8	3	9	2	5
5	2	8	1	7	9	6	3	4
4	3	9	6	5	8	7	1	2
2	7	5	9	4	1	8	6	3
6	8	1	7	3	2	4	5	9
8	4	3	2	1	7	5	9	6
9	5	2	8	6	4	3	7	1
1	6	7	3	9	5	2	4	8

1 2 8

4	2	7	5	9	6	1	8	3
6	3	1	4	8	2	5	9	7
8	9	5	3	7	1	2	4	6
2	4	9	6	1	3	8	7	5
3	1	8	7	4	5	9	6	2
5	7	6	8	2	9	3	1	4
9	8	3	2	6	7	4	5	1
7	5	4	1	3	8	6	2	9
1	6	2	9	5	4	7	3	8

1 2 9

2	5	4	9	7	1	8	3	6
3	7	8	5	6	2	4	9	1
9	1	6	3	8	4	5	2	7
6	4	7	1	5	3	9	8	2
8	2	3	6	9	7	1	5	4
5	9	1	2	4	8	6	7	3
4	8	9	7	3	6	2	1	5
1	3	5	4	2	9	7	6	8
7	6	2	8	1	5	3	4	9

1 3 0

5	8	1	9	2	7	3	6	4
7	2	6	5	3	4	9	8	1
4	9	3	1	6	8	7	5	2
9	3	8	2	4	5	1	7	6
6	1	5	8	7	3	2	4	9
2	4	7	6	1	9	5	3	8
8	7	9	4	5	2	6	1	3
1	5	4	3	9	6	8	2	7
3	6	2	7	8	1	4	9	5

1 3 1

2	8	9	5	7	1	6	4	3
7	1	5	6	3	4	8	2	9
3	6	4	2	8	9	5	7	1
5	3	6	8	2	7	9	1	4
8	9	1	4	6	3	2	5	7
4	2	7	1	9	5	3	8	6
1	4	2	9	5	6	7	3	8
6	7	8	3	4	2	1	9	5
9	5	3	7	1	8	4	6	2

1 3 2

9	1	6	2	3	4	7	8	5
3	7	4	9	8	5	2	1	6
8	2	5	6	1	7	9	4	3
6	4	9	1	2	3	8	5	7
1	3	2	7	5	8	4	6	9
7	5	8	4	6	9	1	3	2
2	8	1	5	7	6	3	9	4
5	9	3	8	4	2	6	7	1
4	6	7	3	9	1	5	2	8

133

3	7	6	9	8	1	5	4	2
4	9	5	7	6	2	1	3	8
2	8	1	4	3	5	9	7	6
7	6	3	1	9	4	2	8	5
9	2	4	5	7	8	3	6	1
5	1	8	3	2	6	4	9	7
1	5	9	6	4	7	8	2	3
8	4	7	2	1	3	6	5	9
6	3	2	8	5	9	7	1	4

134

1	7	6	4	3	2	9	8	5
3	4	2	5	8	9	1	6	7
9	5	8	7	6	1	2	3	4
5	6	4	3	1	7	8	9	2
7	3	1	9	2	8	4	5	6
8	2	9	6	5	4	7	1	3
4	8	5	1	7	6	3	2	9
6	1	7	2	9	3	5	4	8
2	9	3	8	4	5	6	7	1

135

8	5	3	7	6	9	4	2	1
6	1	2	3	8	4	7	5	9
9	4	7	1	2	5	8	6	3
7	8	6	5	3	2	1	9	4
5	3	9	4	1	8	2	7	6
4	2	1	6	9	7	5	3	8
2	9	5	8	4	6	3	1	7
1	6	8	2	7	3	9	4	5
3	7	4	9	5	1	6	8	2

136

4	2	6	1	7	9	5	8	3
8	7	5	4	2	3	9	1	6
3	9	1	5	6	8	2	7	4
5	3	9	6	4	7	1	2	8
2	8	4	3	9	1	6	5	7
6	1	7	2	8	5	4	3	9
9	5	3	8	1	4	7	6	2
1	4	2	7	3	6	8	9	5
7	6	8	9	5	2	3	4	1

137

1	5	7	4	3	8	6	9	2
2	3	9	6	5	1	8	7	4
8	6	4	7	2	9	1	3	5
5	9	8	3	4	2	7	1	6
7	4	1	8	6	5	9	2	3
6	2	3	1	9	7	4	5	8
3	1	5	9	8	4	2	6	7
4	7	6	2	1	3	5	8	9
9	8	2	5	7	6	3	4	1

138

1	2	8	9	5	7	3	6	4
6	9	3	4	8	1	7	5	2
7	4	5	2	6	3	9	1	8
8	3	2	7	1	9	6	4	5
4	5	6	8	3	2	1	9	7
9	1	7	5	4	6	2	8	3
2	6	4	1	7	8	5	3	9
3	8	9	6	2	5	4	7	1
5	7	1	3	9	4	8	2	6

139

1	6	9	5	8	7	3	4	2
8	7	3	9	4	2	1	5	6
5	4	2	6	3	1	8	9	7
2	9	1	4	5	6	7	3	8
3	8	4	7	2	9	6	1	5
6	5	7	3	1	8	4	2	9
9	3	6	1	7	5	2	8	4
4	2	5	8	6	3	9	7	1
7	1	8	2	9	4	5	6	3

140

5	4	2	8	7	6	9	1	3
6	9	3	2	1	4	8	7	5
7	1	8	5	3	9	6	4	2
1	3	7	9	2	8	5	6	4
8	6	4	3	5	1	2	9	7
9	2	5	6	4	7	3	8	1
4	5	6	7	8	2	1	3	9
2	7	9	1	6	3	4	5	8
3	8	1	4	9	5	7	2	6

141

9	2	1	5	8	4	6	3	7
7	4	6	2	1	3	5	8	9
8	5	3	6	9	7	2	1	4
2	6	9	8	7	1	4	5	3
5	3	4	9	2	6	1	7	8
1	8	7	3	4	5	9	2	6
6	9	5	1	3	8	7	4	2
4	1	8	7	6	2	3	9	5
3	7	2	4	5	9	8	6	1

142

5	9	1	8	4	7	3	2	6
3	8	7	2	9	6	5	4	1
4	2	6	5	3	1	7	8	9
2	1	4	9	7	3	8	6	5
6	7	3	4	5	8	9	1	2
8	5	9	6	1	2	4	7	3
1	6	5	7	8	9	2	3	4
9	3	8	1	2	4	6	5	7
7	4	2	3	6	5	1	9	8

143

7	9	6	1	3	4	2	8	5
5	3	4	8	6	2	9	1	7
2	8	1	5	7	9	3	4	6
1	4	7	6	9	8	5	2	3
9	6	5	4	2	3	1	7	8
8	2	3	7	5	1	4	6	9
4	1	9	3	8	7	6	5	2
6	7	2	9	1	5	8	3	4
3	5	8	2	4	6	7	9	1

144

9	2	7	5	8	4	3	1	6
1	8	3	6	7	2	5	4	9
6	5	4	3	9	1	8	7	2
7	3	1	2	4	9	6	8	5
2	4	8	1	5	6	9	3	7
5	6	9	8	3	7	4	2	1
4	1	2	9	6	8	7	5	3
8	9	5	7	2	3	1	6	4
3	7	6	4	1	5	2	9	8

145

7	6	4	5	8	1	9	3	2
1	8	2	7	9	3	4	5	6
3	9	5	4	2	6	7	8	1
5	2	3	8	1	4	6	9	7
6	4	7	2	3	9	8	1	5
9	1	8	6	7	5	3	2	4
8	3	6	1	5	7	2	4	9
4	5	9	3	6	2	1	7	8
2	7	1	9	4	8	5	6	3

146

3	4	8	9	1	7	6	5	2
9	2	6	8	3	5	1	7	4
1	7	5	2	6	4	3	9	8
4	9	3	5	2	6	8	1	7
8	6	1	4	7	9	2	3	5
2	5	7	3	8	1	4	6	9
7	1	4	6	9	2	5	8	3
5	3	9	1	4	8	7	2	6
6	8	2	7	5	3	9	4	1

147

5	3	7	4	1	2	8	9	6
2	1	8	9	5	6	4	3	7
6	4	9	3	7	8	5	2	1
1	7	6	8	3	9	2	4	5
9	5	2	6	4	7	1	8	3
3	8	4	5	2	1	7	6	9
4	9	3	7	8	5	6	1	2
8	2	5	1	6	3	9	7	4
7	6	1	2	9	4	3	5	8

148

3	5	4	7	9	2	1	8	6
6	7	2	4	1	8	9	3	5
1	8	9	6	5	3	4	2	7
9	1	6	3	7	4	2	5	8
8	2	5	1	6	9	3	7	4
7	4	3	8	2	5	6	1	9
5	3	7	9	4	1	8	6	2
4	6	8	2	3	7	5	9	1
2	9	1	5	8	6	7	4	3

149

2	5	3	6	8	7	4	9	1
6	7	1	5	9	4	8	2	3
4	8	9	2	3	1	5	7	6
9	3	2	1	7	5	6	4	8
8	1	5	9	4	6	7	3	2
7	6	4	8	2	3	9	1	5
1	4	7	3	5	8	2	6	9
3	2	8	4	6	9	1	5	7
5	9	6	7	1	2	3	8	4

150

1	2	7	4	3	5	8	6	9
9	5	6	1	2	8	4	3	7
4	3	8	9	6	7	5	1	2
6	4	3	2	7	9	1	8	5
5	1	2	8	4	6	7	9	3
8	7	9	3	5	1	6	2	4
2	6	4	7	1	3	9	5	8
3	9	5	6	8	4	2	7	1
7	8	1	5	9	2	3	4	6

151

4	3	9	2	5	1	6	8	7
2	6	5	3	7	8	4	1	9
1	8	7	6	9	4	3	5	2
7	9	3	8	1	2	5	6	4
6	5	4	9	3	7	8	2	1
8	2	1	4	6	5	9	7	3
5	1	8	7	4	3	2	9	6
3	7	6	5	2	9	1	4	8
9	4	2	1	8	6	7	3	5

152

1	7	4	6	5	8	2	9	3
8	5	6	9	2	3	7	1	4
2	3	9	4	1	7	5	6	8
6	2	5	8	7	4	1	3	9
4	1	8	5	3	9	6	7	2
7	9	3	1	6	2	8	4	5
3	6	2	7	9	5	4	8	1
9	4	7	2	8	1	3	5	6
5	8	1	3	4	6	9	2	7

153

2	8	7	3	4	5	1	9	6
1	6	4	8	7	9	2	3	5
5	3	9	1	6	2	8	4	7
8	1	3	2	5	6	4	7	9
4	5	2	9	1	7	6	8	3
9	7	6	4	3	8	5	1	2
3	2	1	5	9	4	7	6	8
7	4	5	6	8	3	9	2	1
6	9	8	7	2	1	3	5	4

154

7	6	8	5	9	4	3	1	2
1	2	3	7	8	6	5	4	9
5	9	4	3	2	1	8	7	6
8	1	5	2	7	9	6	3	4
9	7	2	4	6	3	1	8	5
4	3	6	1	5	8	9	2	7
2	5	9	8	1	7	4	6	3
3	8	7	6	4	5	2	9	1
6	4	1	9	3	2	7	5	8

155

3	6	1	2	9	5	7	8	4
2	4	5	6	8	7	9	3	1
9	8	7	4	1	3	5	2	6
1	7	2	3	4	6	8	5	9
8	9	4	1	5	2	3	6	7
5	3	6	9	7	8	1	4	2
7	1	8	5	6	4	2	9	3
4	5	3	7	2	9	6	1	8
6	2	9	8	3	1	4	7	5

156

3	4	7	6	5	8	9	1	2
6	1	5	4	9	2	7	8	3
9	8	2	7	3	1	4	5	6
1	2	8	3	6	4	5	9	7
7	5	3	1	8	9	2	6	4
4	9	6	5	2	7	1	3	8
8	7	4	9	1	3	6	2	5
2	6	9	8	7	5	3	4	1
5	3	1	2	4	6	8	7	9

157

3	8	9	4	2	1	6	5	7
1	4	2	6	5	7	8	9	3
7	5	6	8	3	9	2	1	4
8	3	4	2	1	6	5	7	9
9	7	1	3	8	5	4	6	2
6	2	5	7	9	4	3	8	1
2	9	7	5	6	3	1	4	8
5	1	8	9	4	2	7	3	6
4	6	3	1	7	8	9	2	5

158

2	1	3	7	6	4	5	9	8
6	4	9	3	5	8	2	7	1
8	5	7	9	1	2	4	3	6
7	2	8	4	9	6	1	5	3
9	3	4	1	8	5	7	6	2
5	6	1	2	7	3	9	8	4
3	7	5	6	2	1	8	4	9
4	9	2	8	3	7	6	1	5
1	8	6	5	4	9	3	2	7

159

2	3	4	1	5	8	9	7	6
9	8	1	6	3	7	5	2	4
5	7	6	4	2	9	3	8	1
1	4	5	3	9	2	7	6	8
8	9	2	5	7	6	4	1	3
3	6	7	8	1	4	2	9	5
4	2	3	9	8	1	6	5	7
7	5	8	2	6	3	1	4	9
6	1	9	7	4	5	8	3	2

160

4	1	7	8	6	5	9	3	2
9	6	3	7	1	2	4	5	8
8	5	2	4	3	9	1	6	7
7	2	1	6	5	8	3	4	9
5	4	9	1	2	3	7	8	6
3	8	6	9	4	7	2	1	5
1	3	8	2	9	6	5	7	4
2	7	5	3	8	4	6	9	1
6	9	4	5	7	1	8	2	3

161

1	3	4	9	8	5	2	6	7
9	8	2	3	6	7	5	4	1
6	7	5	2	4	1	8	9	3
3	5	1	4	2	9	6	7	8
2	4	9	6	7	8	3	1	5
8	6	7	1	5	3	9	2	4
4	9	8	7	3	2	1	5	6
7	2	3	5	1	6	4	8	9
5	1	6	8	9	4	7	3	2

162

9	4	6	5	7	2	3	1	8
7	5	1	6	8	3	9	4	2
3	8	2	4	9	1	5	7	6
6	9	8	2	4	5	1	3	7
5	2	7	3	1	8	4	6	9
4	1	3	9	6	7	2	8	5
1	3	9	8	5	6	7	2	4
8	7	4	1	2	9	6	5	3
2	6	5	7	3	4	8	9	1

163

3	8	7	9	4	6	2	5	1
4	5	2	3	1	7	6	9	8
6	1	9	5	8	2	3	4	7
9	3	5	1	7	8	4	6	2
1	6	4	2	9	3	7	8	5
7	2	8	4	6	5	9	1	3
8	4	6	7	3	1	5	2	9
5	7	1	6	2	9	8	3	4
2	9	3	8	5	4	1	7	6

164

7	2	6	8	4	9	1	5	3
8	9	5	1	3	2	6	4	7
4	3	1	5	6	7	9	8	2
9	7	3	6	5	1	8	2	4
6	5	2	9	8	4	7	3	1
1	4	8	2	7	3	5	6	9
2	8	4	7	9	5	3	1	6
3	6	9	4	1	8	2	7	5
5	1	7	3	2	6	4	9	8

165

5	7	8	3	2	4	6	9	1
6	4	1	7	5	9	2	8	3
9	3	2	8	1	6	7	5	4
2	5	9	4	3	7	1	6	8
1	8	7	2	6	5	4	3	9
3	6	4	1	9	8	5	2	7
4	9	6	5	7	3	8	1	2
7	1	5	9	8	2	3	4	6
8	2	3	6	4	1	9	7	5

166

5	2	8	7	1	3	9	6	4
6	9	7	2	4	8	5	1	3
1	4	3	5	6	9	7	8	2
4	3	1	9	8	7	2	5	6
8	5	9	3	2	6	4	7	1
7	6	2	1	5	4	8	3	9
2	8	6	4	7	1	3	9	5
9	1	4	8	3	5	6	2	7
3	7	5	6	9	2	1	4	8

167

1	6	8	2	7	4	3	9	5
7	4	2	9	3	5	8	6	1
3	9	5	6	8	1	2	4	7
9	7	1	3	2	8	6	5	4
5	2	3	7	4	6	9	1	8
6	8	4	1	5	9	7	3	2
4	5	9	8	6	2	1	7	3
8	3	6	5	1	7	4	2	9
2	1	7	4	9	3	5	8	6

168

4	7	6	9	2	1	8	5	3
8	3	5	6	4	7	9	2	1
2	1	9	8	5	3	4	7	6
7	2	1	5	8	6	3	9	4
5	8	4	1	3	9	7	6	2
9	6	3	4	7	2	5	1	8
6	9	8	3	1	5	2	4	7
3	5	2	7	6	4	1	8	9
1	4	7	2	9	8	6	3	5

169

2	9	8	3	1	5	6	4	7
6	4	5	7	2	9	1	3	8
7	1	3	8	4	6	5	9	2
8	5	1	6	7	4	9	2	3
3	7	2	9	8	1	4	6	5
9	6	4	2	5	3	8	7	1
5	8	6	4	3	2	7	1	9
1	2	9	5	6	7	3	8	4
4	3	7	1	9	8	2	5	6

170

5	9	2	4	8	7	6	3	1
4	7	8	1	6	3	5	9	2
1	3	6	5	9	2	4	7	8
7	2	5	9	3	8	1	4	6
3	8	1	6	4	5	9	2	7
6	4	9	7	2	1	8	5	3
8	1	4	2	7	9	3	6	5
2	6	3	8	5	4	7	1	9
9	5	7	3	1	6	2	8	4

171

6	7	2	3	9	5	4	8	1
3	1	5	4	8	2	9	6	7
9	8	4	7	1	6	2	5	3
5	9	3	8	4	1	6	7	2
1	2	6	5	7	9	8	3	4
8	4	7	6	2	3	5	1	9
4	3	8	9	6	7	1	2	5
7	6	1	2	5	4	3	9	8
2	5	9	1	3	8	7	4	6

172

2	1	4	9	8	3	6	5	7
6	7	9	5	4	2	8	3	1
8	3	5	1	7	6	9	4	2
3	8	2	4	1	7	5	9	6
5	6	1	2	3	9	7	8	4
9	4	7	6	5	8	2	1	3
1	2	6	3	9	5	4	7	8
4	9	8	7	6	1	3	2	5
7	5	3	8	2	4	1	6	9

173

6	4	9	3	2	8	1	7	5
7	5	1	6	9	4	8	3	2
3	2	8	7	1	5	6	9	4
2	1	3	8	6	9	4	5	7
4	9	6	1	5	7	3	2	8
5	8	7	2	4	3	9	6	1
1	3	5	9	8	2	7	4	6
9	6	4	5	7	1	2	8	3
8	7	2	4	3	6	5	1	9

174

9	7	4	2	8	1	5	3	6
3	6	2	5	4	9	7	8	1
1	5	8	7	3	6	4	2	9
2	1	6	3	7	8	9	5	4
4	8	7	6	9	5	3	1	2
5	3	9	4	1	2	6	7	8
6	2	1	9	5	3	8	4	7
8	4	5	1	6	7	2	9	3
7	9	3	8	2	4	1	6	5

175

4	5	2	7	9	1	3	8	6
3	7	1	8	5	6	9	2	4
9	6	8	3	2	4	1	5	7
8	3	5	9	1	7	4	6	2
6	4	9	2	8	5	7	1	3
2	1	7	4	6	3	5	9	8
7	2	6	5	3	9	8	4	1
5	8	4	1	7	2	6	3	9
1	9	3	6	4	8	2	7	5

176

1	5	9	8	3	2	6	4	7
6	7	3	9	4	5	8	2	1
4	8	2	1	7	6	5	3	9
8	1	6	7	5	3	2	9	4
5	9	7	4	2	1	3	6	8
3	2	4	6	9	8	7	1	5
9	4	5	3	6	7	1	8	2
7	6	1	2	8	4	9	5	3
2	3	8	5	1	9	4	7	6

177

1	6	5	2	7	8	4	3	9
9	4	8	6	5	3	1	7	2
3	7	2	1	9	4	5	6	8
5	8	6	7	4	9	2	1	3
4	1	7	3	6	2	9	8	5
2	9	3	5	8	1	7	4	6
7	2	1	9	3	6	8	5	4
6	5	4	8	2	7	3	9	1
8	3	9	4	1	5	6	2	7

178

3	6	5	2	1	9	8	7	4
4	1	7	6	5	8	3	9	2
8	2	9	7	4	3	6	5	1
7	4	2	3	6	1	9	8	5
9	3	6	4	8	5	1	2	7
1	5	8	9	7	2	4	3	6
2	9	1	5	3	4	7	6	8
6	8	3	1	2	7	5	4	9
5	7	4	8	9	6	2	1	3

179

3	5	7	8	2	9	4	1	6
1	9	8	5	6	4	7	2	3
4	2	6	3	1	7	9	8	5
2	4	1	9	5	3	8	6	7
9	7	5	6	4	8	2	3	1
6	8	3	2	7	1	5	4	9
5	6	4	7	3	2	1	9	8
7	1	9	4	8	6	3	5	2
8	3	2	1	9	5	6	7	4

180

5	4	9	6	7	3	1	2	8
2	6	7	8	5	1	3	4	9
3	8	1	9	4	2	7	5	6
1	2	6	3	9	8	5	7	4
4	7	3	2	6	5	8	9	1
9	5	8	4	1	7	2	6	3
6	3	2	5	8	4	9	1	7
7	9	5	1	3	6	4	8	2
8	1	4	7	2	9	6	3	5

181

5	3	9	4	1	2	8	6	7
8	1	7	9	6	5	2	3	4
2	6	4	7	8	3	9	5	1
4	2	1	3	9	8	6	7	5
3	9	5	1	7	6	4	8	2
6	7	8	2	5	4	1	9	3
1	5	2	6	3	9	7	4	8
9	4	3	8	2	7	5	1	6
7	8	6	5	4	1	3	2	9

182

1	6	4	9	2	7	5	8	3
2	3	5	1	4	8	7	9	6
8	7	9	3	5	6	2	1	4
9	5	8	7	6	2	3	4	1
7	2	3	4	1	9	8	6	5
6	4	1	5	8	3	9	2	7
3	8	2	6	7	4	1	5	9
4	1	7	2	9	5	6	3	8
5	9	6	8	3	1	4	7	2

183

6	4	3	2	7	5	1	9	8
9	1	2	8	3	6	5	7	4
7	8	5	1	4	9	3	2	6
2	9	7	4	5	3	6	8	1
8	6	4	7	1	2	9	5	3
5	3	1	6	9	8	2	4	7
4	7	9	5	6	1	8	3	2
3	2	6	9	8	7	4	1	5
1	5	8	3	2	4	7	6	9

184

5	3	6	9	7	1	8	2	4
2	8	7	5	3	4	1	9	6
1	9	4	6	8	2	7	3	5
8	1	9	3	2	5	6	4	7
6	5	2	1	4	7	3	8	9
7	4	3	8	9	6	2	5	1
4	6	8	2	1	9	5	7	3
9	2	5	7	6	3	4	1	8
3	7	1	4	5	8	9	6	2

185

8	9	4	5	2	1	3	7	6
3	1	2	9	6	7	4	8	5
6	5	7	8	3	4	9	2	1
2	4	5	7	8	6	1	9	3
9	3	1	4	5	2	7	6	8
7	6	8	1	9	3	5	4	2
1	8	3	6	4	9	2	5	7
4	7	6	2	1	5	8	3	9
5	2	9	3	7	8	6	1	4

186

4	6	3	7	5	2	8	1	9
1	8	7	6	4	9	5	2	3
2	9	5	1	8	3	7	4	6
9	7	6	5	3	4	2	8	1
3	1	4	8	2	6	9	5	7
8	5	2	9	7	1	6	3	4
6	3	9	2	1	8	4	7	5
5	4	8	3	6	7	1	9	2
7	2	1	4	9	5	3	6	8

187

1	6	7	9	2	4	5	3	8
4	9	8	7	5	3	6	2	1
3	5	2	8	1	6	4	7	9
5	3	6	4	7	8	9	1	2
9	2	4	1	3	5	8	6	7
8	7	1	2	6	9	3	4	5
7	8	9	3	4	2	1	5	6
2	4	5	6	9	1	7	8	3
6	1	3	5	8	7	2	9	4

188

5	2	8	3	4	1	6	9	7
4	3	9	6	7	5	2	8	1
6	1	7	8	9	2	3	5	4
1	8	6	7	3	9	5	4	2
9	7	5	4	2	8	1	6	3
2	4	3	5	1	6	8	7	9
3	5	4	1	8	7	9	2	6
8	9	1	2	6	4	7	3	5
7	6	2	9	5	3	4	1	8

189

8	2	4	9	3	7	5	6	1
7	5	9	2	6	1	8	4	3
6	3	1	8	5	4	7	2	9
2	4	7	3	1	6	9	8	5
5	8	3	4	7	9	6	1	2
1	9	6	5	8	2	4	3	7
9	7	2	1	4	8	3	5	6
3	6	8	7	2	5	1	9	4
4	1	5	6	9	3	2	7	8

190

3	4	1	7	9	2	6	5	8
2	9	7	8	5	6	1	3	4
5	6	8	3	1	4	7	2	9
4	1	9	6	3	8	5	7	2
7	2	6	1	4	5	8	9	3
8	5	3	9	2	7	4	1	6
6	7	5	2	8	3	9	4	1
9	8	2	4	7	1	3	6	5
1	3	4	5	6	9	2	8	7

191

2	1	6	3	5	4	8	9	7
8	3	5	1	9	7	2	4	6
4	9	7	6	2	8	1	5	3
5	7	9	2	4	3	6	1	8
6	4	2	7	8	1	9	3	5
1	8	3	5	6	9	7	2	4
7	2	4	8	1	5	3	6	9
3	5	1	9	7	6	4	8	2
9	6	8	4	3	2	5	7	1

192

9	4	8	7	2	3	6	1	5
5	1	7	8	9	6	4	2	3
3	6	2	5	4	1	7	8	9
4	2	3	9	7	8	5	6	1
7	8	9	6	1	5	3	4	2
1	5	6	4	3	2	8	9	7
8	9	4	2	5	7	1	3	6
6	7	1	3	8	9	2	5	4
2	3	5	1	6	4	9	7	8

193

4	7	9	6	3	1	2	5	8
6	2	3	5	7	8	1	9	4
8	1	5	2	9	4	3	7	6
1	6	7	3	4	5	8	2	9
9	5	8	1	2	6	4	3	7
2	3	4	9	8	7	6	1	5
5	4	6	7	1	3	9	8	2
7	9	1	8	6	2	5	4	3
3	8	2	4	5	9	7	6	1

194

2	3	6	1	9	5	4	7	8
4	1	8	6	2	7	5	3	9
7	5	9	3	4	8	1	2	6
6	7	5	8	1	4	3	9	2
9	8	4	5	3	2	6	1	7
1	2	3	7	6	9	8	4	5
5	6	2	4	7	3	9	8	1
3	9	1	2	8	6	7	5	4
8	4	7	9	5	1	2	6	3

195

3	2	7	8	9	6	5	1	4
6	4	1	2	5	3	7	8	9
9	5	8	4	1	7	2	3	6
4	8	9	1	6	2	3	5	7
1	7	6	9	3	5	4	2	8
5	3	2	7	8	4	9	6	1
2	6	4	5	7	1	8	9	3
8	1	5	3	4	9	6	7	2
7	9	3	6	2	8	1	4	5

196

2	1	9	7	6	5	3	4	8
5	3	6	2	8	4	9	7	1
7	4	8	1	3	9	6	2	5
6	5	1	4	7	3	8	9	2
3	2	4	8	9	6	5	1	7
8	9	7	5	2	1	4	6	3
4	6	2	3	5	7	1	8	9
9	7	5	6	1	8	2	3	4
1	8	3	9	4	2	7	5	6

197

9	7	5	4	2	6	3	8	1
4	8	2	9	3	1	7	5	6
3	1	6	8	5	7	2	4	9
1	2	9	3	6	8	4	7	5
6	4	3	7	9	5	1	2	8
8	5	7	2	1	4	9	6	3
7	3	1	6	8	2	5	9	4
5	6	4	1	7	9	8	3	2
2	9	8	5	4	3	6	1	7

198

4	8	6	9	1	7	3	2	5
9	2	5	8	3	6	7	1	4
1	3	7	5	2	4	8	6	9
3	5	9	6	4	2	1	7	8
7	1	8	3	9	5	6	4	2
2	6	4	1	7	8	9	5	3
8	9	2	7	5	1	4	3	6
5	7	3	4	6	9	2	8	1
6	4	1	2	8	3	5	9	7

199

1	9	4	6	8	5	7	3	2
5	6	7	2	4	3	1	9	8
2	8	3	9	7	1	6	5	4
9	3	1	5	6	2	8	4	7
7	5	2	4	9	8	3	1	6
6	4	8	1	3	7	5	2	9
4	7	6	3	1	9	2	8	5
8	1	5	7	2	4	9	6	3
3	2	9	8	5	6	4	7	1

200

6	8	5	4	3	7	1	9	2
7	4	9	1	5	2	8	6	3
2	3	1	6	8	9	4	7	5
1	9	8	5	6	4	2	3	7
3	6	7	9	2	8	5	4	1
5	2	4	3	7	1	6	8	9
4	7	2	8	9	5	3	1	6
9	1	3	2	4	6	7	5	8
8	5	6	7	1	3	9	2	4

201

3	2	9	4	5	6	1	8	7
4	1	5	3	7	8	2	9	6
6	8	7	2	9	1	3	5	4
2	5	1	9	6	3	4	7	8
7	4	3	5	8	2	9	6	1
8	9	6	7	1	4	5	3	2
9	7	2	8	4	5	6	1	3
1	3	8	6	2	9	7	4	5
5	6	4	1	3	7	8	2	9

202

3	9	2	7	4	6	1	5	8
5	6	8	2	9	1	7	3	4
1	4	7	8	3	5	2	9	6
7	5	4	9	6	8	3	2	1
2	3	9	4	1	7	8	6	5
8	1	6	3	5	2	9	4	7
4	8	5	1	2	3	6	7	9
6	7	3	5	8	9	4	1	2
9	2	1	6	7	4	5	8	3

203

7	9	2	8	4	3	5	1	6
8	3	6	7	1	5	9	4	2
5	4	1	2	6	9	3	8	7
2	6	4	3	9	8	7	5	1
1	7	8	4	5	6	2	9	3
9	5	3	1	7	2	4	6	8
6	1	5	9	2	7	8	3	4
3	2	9	6	8	4	1	7	5
4	8	7	5	3	1	6	2	9

204

9	2	4	7	6	5	1	3	8
7	1	8	4	2	3	9	5	6
3	6	5	1	9	8	2	4	7
1	8	2	6	3	7	5	9	4
4	5	9	2	8	1	7	6	3
6	7	3	9	5	4	8	2	1
8	4	6	5	1	9	3	7	2
5	3	7	8	4	2	6	1	9
2	9	1	3	7	6	4	8	5

205

```
7 9 2 3 6 1 5 8 4
8 1 4 7 9 5 2 6 3
6 3 5 8 4 2 9 1 7
4 5 8 2 3 6 1 7 9
3 7 9 1 8 4 6 5 2
1 2 6 9 5 7 4 3 8
2 8 1 5 7 9 3 4 6
9 6 7 4 1 3 8 2 5
5 4 3 6 2 8 7 9 1
```

206

```
6 7 3 1 8 4 9 2 5
4 1 2 6 9 5 3 8 7
8 5 9 2 3 7 1 6 4
2 8 5 4 1 6 7 3 9
7 6 4 9 5 3 2 1 8
9 3 1 7 2 8 5 4 6
3 9 7 8 6 2 4 5 1
1 2 6 5 4 9 8 7 3
5 4 8 3 7 1 6 9 2
```

207

```
6 2 9 1 3 4 5 8 7
3 4 7 9 8 5 6 2 1
8 5 1 6 7 2 9 4 3
1 8 5 3 2 9 7 6 4
4 6 2 7 1 8 3 5 9
7 9 3 5 4 6 2 1 8
2 3 8 4 5 7 1 9 6
5 7 6 8 9 1 4 3 2
9 1 4 2 6 3 8 7 5
```

208

```
6 1 4 7 8 9 3 5 2
9 8 2 6 5 3 1 4 7
3 5 7 4 2 1 8 6 9
8 6 1 2 4 7 5 9 3
5 7 9 3 6 8 2 1 4
2 4 3 1 9 5 7 8 6
1 2 5 9 7 4 6 3 8
7 9 8 5 3 6 4 2 1
4 3 6 8 1 2 9 7 5
```

209

```
4 7 9 3 8 5 1 2 6
6 2 5 7 4 1 9 8 3
8 1 3 2 9 6 7 5 4
9 4 1 5 2 7 3 6 8
7 6 2 8 3 4 5 1 9
5 3 8 6 1 9 4 7 2
2 5 4 1 6 3 8 9 7
3 8 7 9 5 2 6 4 1
1 9 6 4 7 8 2 3 5
```

210

```
5 1 6 4 7 3 8 2 9
7 9 2 6 8 1 4 5 3
4 8 3 2 5 9 1 6 7
1 6 5 7 4 8 9 3 2
8 3 4 5 9 2 7 1 6
9 2 7 1 3 6 5 8 4
6 5 1 9 2 4 3 7 8
3 7 9 8 6 5 2 4 1
2 4 8 3 1 7 6 9 5
```

211

```
5 1 7 3 6 2 4 8 9
6 9 8 7 1 4 2 3 5
4 2 3 5 8 9 7 1 6
1 7 6 4 5 8 3 9 2
8 5 9 6 2 3 1 4 7
3 4 2 9 7 1 5 6 8
9 6 4 2 3 7 8 5 1
7 8 5 1 4 6 9 2 3
2 3 1 8 9 5 6 7 4
```

212

```
5 7 6 3 4 1 2 9 8
1 9 8 5 2 6 4 7 3
3 2 4 9 7 8 6 1 5
2 4 9 1 8 5 7 3 6
7 6 1 4 9 3 5 8 2
8 5 3 7 6 2 1 4 9
4 8 5 2 3 7 9 6 1
9 3 2 6 1 4 8 5 7
6 1 7 8 5 9 3 2 4
```

213

```
7 4 1 5 6 8 3 2 9
9 8 3 7 2 1 4 6 5
6 5 2 3 9 4 7 8 1
5 6 9 1 4 7 8 3 2
3 1 4 6 8 2 5 9 7
8 2 7 9 5 3 1 4 6
1 7 6 4 3 9 2 5 8
2 3 5 8 7 6 9 1 4
4 9 8 2 1 5 6 7 3
```

214

```
3 5 7 2 6 4 9 1 8
6 1 9 7 8 3 2 5 4
8 2 4 5 9 1 3 7 6
1 3 6 9 5 8 7 4 2
7 9 2 3 4 6 1 8 5
4 8 5 1 2 7 6 9 3
2 6 8 4 7 9 5 3 1
9 4 1 6 3 5 8 2 7
5 7 3 8 1 2 4 6 9
```

215

```
3 5 7 4 6 8 9 1 2
6 9 2 5 3 1 7 8 4
4 1 8 7 9 2 6 3 5
5 7 9 8 4 6 1 2 3
8 6 3 2 1 7 4 5 9
1 2 4 3 5 9 8 7 6
9 8 5 1 2 4 3 6 7
7 3 6 9 8 5 2 4 1
2 4 1 6 7 3 5 9 8
```

216

```
9 4 1 8 3 7 6 5 2
3 7 8 5 2 6 9 4 1
2 6 5 9 1 4 3 7 8
8 5 4 7 9 1 2 3 6
7 1 9 2 6 3 4 8 5
6 3 2 4 5 8 7 1 9
5 8 3 6 4 2 1 9 7
4 2 7 1 8 9 5 6 3
1 9 6 3 7 5 8 2 4
```

217

1	3	8	2	7	4	5	6	9
6	2	7	1	9	5	4	3	8
4	9	5	3	8	6	1	2	7
5	6	3	4	2	9	7	8	1
8	7	4	6	1	3	9	5	2
9	1	2	7	5	8	6	4	3
3	8	1	5	6	7	2	9	4
7	5	9	8	4	2	3	1	6
2	4	6	9	3	1	8	7	5

218

4	7	5	8	2	3	1	9	6
2	6	3	9	5	1	4	8	7
1	8	9	4	6	7	5	2	3
6	4	7	3	1	2	8	5	9
3	5	8	7	4	9	2	6	1
9	2	1	6	8	5	7	3	4
7	9	2	1	3	8	6	4	5
5	3	6	2	7	4	9	1	8
8	1	4	5	9	6	3	7	2

219

2	9	3	1	6	8	5	4	7
4	5	7	9	3	2	6	1	8
1	8	6	4	7	5	9	3	2
9	2	5	6	1	4	8	7	3
3	4	1	7	8	9	2	6	5
7	6	8	2	5	3	4	9	1
5	3	4	8	9	7	1	2	6
8	1	2	3	4	6	7	5	9
6	7	9	5	2	1	3	8	4

220

2	8	3	1	4	9	5	7	6
5	1	4	2	6	7	8	9	3
6	7	9	3	8	5	2	4	1
8	5	6	4	3	1	7	2	9
7	9	2	8	5	6	1	3	4
3	4	1	7	9	2	6	8	5
4	3	7	5	1	8	9	6	2
9	2	5	6	7	4	3	1	8
1	6	8	9	2	3	4	5	7

221

2	5	8	7	6	4	1	9	3
4	6	3	1	2	9	8	5	7
1	9	7	8	5	3	4	2	6
7	1	9	6	8	5	3	4	2
5	2	4	3	7	1	9	6	8
8	3	6	9	4	2	5	7	1
6	7	1	5	9	8	2	3	4
9	8	2	4	3	7	6	1	5
3	4	5	2	1	6	7	8	9

222

6	7	4	9	8	3	1	5	2
5	1	2	6	4	7	8	9	3
9	8	3	5	2	1	7	4	6
1	2	8	4	5	6	3	7	9
3	9	5	2	7	8	4	6	1
7	4	6	1	3	9	2	8	5
4	5	9	8	1	2	6	3	7
8	3	1	7	6	5	9	2	4
2	6	7	3	9	4	5	1	8

223

6	5	9	4	1	7	2	8	3
7	8	1	5	3	2	6	4	9
2	4	3	9	6	8	5	1	7
4	2	7	8	9	6	3	5	1
5	3	6	2	7	1	8	9	4
9	1	8	3	5	4	7	6	2
1	7	5	6	2	9	4	3	8
8	6	2	1	4	3	9	7	5
3	9	4	7	8	5	1	2	6

224

8	7	5	1	4	2	9	3	6
3	2	9	5	7	6	8	1	4
4	1	6	9	8	3	7	5	2
7	9	1	8	6	4	3	2	5
6	3	2	7	9	5	4	8	1
5	4	8	2	3	1	6	9	7
2	6	3	4	5	9	1	7	8
1	8	4	3	2	7	5	6	9
9	5	7	6	1	8	2	4	3

225

4	8	6	7	3	5	1	2	9
3	9	2	1	6	4	8	5	7
1	5	7	2	8	9	4	6	3
5	3	4	6	7	2	9	8	1
6	7	1	5	9	8	3	4	2
9	2	8	4	1	3	6	7	5
2	6	5	9	4	1	7	3	8
7	1	3	8	2	6	5	9	4
8	4	9	3	5	7	2	1	6

226

9	7	6	5	2	8	1	4	3
3	4	5	9	7	1	2	8	6
8	1	2	4	3	6	9	5	7
5	6	3	1	9	4	8	7	2
2	8	4	7	5	3	6	1	9
1	9	7	6	8	2	5	3	4
6	3	9	8	1	7	4	2	5
4	2	8	3	6	5	7	9	1
7	5	1	2	4	9	3	6	8

227

2	3	1	7	9	8	5	6	4
6	5	8	1	4	2	7	3	9
4	9	7	5	3	6	8	2	1
5	2	9	6	7	4	1	8	3
8	7	6	2	1	3	4	9	5
1	4	3	8	5	9	2	7	6
7	1	2	9	6	5	3	4	8
9	8	4	3	2	1	6	5	7
3	6	5	4	8	7	9	1	2

228

3	7	8	2	5	9	4	1	6
2	4	1	7	6	3	9	8	5
9	6	5	8	4	1	3	7	2
8	1	7	4	2	5	6	9	3
6	3	4	1	9	8	5	2	7
5	9	2	6	3	7	1	4	8
4	5	6	9	8	2	7	3	1
7	8	3	5	1	4	2	6	9
1	2	9	3	7	6	8	5	4

229

5	2	3	6	7	9	4	8	1
7	1	4	2	8	3	5	9	6
8	9	6	5	1	4	3	7	2
4	7	5	1	9	8	2	6	3
6	3	2	7	4	5	9	1	8
9	8	1	3	2	6	7	4	5
2	5	7	9	6	1	8	3	4
3	6	8	4	5	7	1	2	9
1	4	9	8	3	2	6	5	7

230

8	6	9	5	1	2	4	7	3
2	3	4	8	6	7	1	9	5
1	7	5	9	3	4	6	2	8
7	1	2	4	8	3	9	5	6
5	9	3	2	7	6	8	4	1
4	8	6	1	9	5	2	3	7
6	4	8	7	5	9	3	1	2
3	2	7	6	4	1	5	8	9
9	5	1	3	2	8	7	6	4

231

2	5	9	6	7	8	4	3	1
8	3	1	4	9	5	6	7	2
4	7	6	1	2	3	8	9	5
9	6	7	5	1	4	2	8	3
1	4	8	2	3	6	9	5	7
5	2	3	7	8	9	1	4	6
6	9	2	8	5	7	3	1	4
3	1	5	9	4	2	7	6	8
7	8	4	3	6	1	5	2	9

232

6	5	1	3	8	7	2	9	4
3	7	9	5	2	4	8	1	6
4	2	8	6	1	9	3	5	7
8	9	5	7	4	3	1	6	2
1	4	6	8	5	2	7	3	9
2	3	7	1	9	6	5	4	8
5	8	2	4	6	1	9	7	3
7	1	4	9	3	8	6	2	5
9	6	3	2	7	5	4	8	1

233

1	9	4	3	2	5	7	6	8
8	6	5	4	9	7	3	1	2
3	7	2	1	8	6	9	4	5
4	1	8	2	3	9	5	7	6
9	5	6	7	4	8	2	3	1
7	2	3	5	6	1	8	9	4
2	8	9	6	7	4	1	5	3
6	3	1	9	5	2	4	8	7
5	4	7	8	1	3	6	2	9

234

1	3	2	7	4	6	5	8	9
8	9	6	1	5	2	4	7	3
4	5	7	9	8	3	1	6	2
9	2	4	8	7	1	3	5	6
7	6	8	5	3	9	2	1	4
3	1	5	2	6	4	7	9	8
5	4	3	6	1	8	9	2	7
2	8	1	3	9	7	6	4	5
6	7	9	4	2	5	8	3	1

235

9	4	6	2	1	7	5	8	3
2	7	8	9	5	3	6	4	1
5	3	1	6	4	8	2	7	9
1	8	4	3	9	2	7	5	6
7	9	2	4	6	5	3	1	8
6	5	3	8	7	1	4	9	2
3	2	7	1	8	4	9	6	5
4	1	9	5	3	6	8	2	7
8	6	5	7	2	9	1	3	4

236

6	3	5	2	9	1	4	7	8
8	9	1	4	3	7	2	6	5
7	2	4	5	6	8	9	1	3
5	1	6	9	2	3	8	4	7
4	8	2	7	1	5	3	9	6
9	7	3	6	8	4	1	5	2
2	6	8	1	5	9	7	3	4
3	4	9	8	7	6	5	2	1
1	5	7	3	4	2	6	8	9

237

5	4	1	7	8	6	2	3	9
9	8	3	5	4	2	7	6	1
2	7	6	9	3	1	5	8	4
1	2	7	6	9	4	8	5	3
6	9	5	3	2	8	1	4	7
8	3	4	1	5	7	6	9	2
4	6	8	2	1	3	9	7	5
3	5	2	8	7	9	4	1	6
7	1	9	4	6	5	3	2	8

238

5	1	2	6	3	4	7	8	9
7	4	3	9	5	8	6	1	2
6	8	9	1	2	7	4	3	5
9	5	6	3	1	2	8	4	7
4	7	1	5	8	9	3	2	6
2	3	8	4	7	6	9	5	1
8	6	4	2	9	5	1	7	3
1	2	7	8	6	3	5	9	4
3	9	5	7	4	1	2	6	8

239

4	1	3	5	7	6	2	9	8
7	2	6	4	9	8	5	3	1
5	9	8	3	1	2	7	6	4
2	5	9	6	4	1	3	8	7
1	8	7	2	5	3	6	4	9
6	3	4	9	8	7	1	5	2
9	7	1	8	3	5	4	2	6
8	6	5	1	2	4	9	7	3
3	4	2	7	6	9	8	1	5

240

2	9	4	7	8	5	6	1	3
1	3	6	4	2	9	8	5	7
7	5	8	6	3	1	4	9	2
4	1	2	9	5	7	3	8	6
6	8	5	2	4	3	1	7	9
3	7	9	1	6	8	5	2	4
5	4	3	8	7	2	9	6	1
9	6	7	5	1	4	2	3	8
8	2	1	3	9	6	7	4	5

2 4 1

6	7	9	4	8	1	5	3	2
4	2	3	6	5	9	1	7	8
1	8	5	3	2	7	6	4	9
3	4	6	2	1	5	8	9	7
8	1	7	9	3	6	4	2	5
5	9	2	7	4	8	3	6	1
2	3	8	5	7	4	9	1	6
7	6	1	8	9	3	2	5	4
9	5	4	1	6	2	7	8	3

2 4 2

3	5	4	9	1	8	6	2	7
9	6	2	5	3	7	1	4	8
8	7	1	4	2	6	9	5	3
7	9	5	6	4	3	8	1	2
6	2	8	1	9	5	3	7	4
4	1	3	8	7	2	5	9	6
5	4	6	7	8	9	2	3	1
1	3	9	2	6	4	7	8	5
2	8	7	3	5	1	4	6	9

2 4 3

8	5	3	2	7	9	6	4	1
6	4	9	8	3	1	2	5	7
2	1	7	4	6	5	8	9	3
5	3	1	7	4	8	9	2	6
4	7	8	9	2	6	1	3	5
9	6	2	1	5	3	4	7	8
7	2	6	3	8	4	5	1	9
1	8	4	5	9	7	3	6	2
3	9	5	6	1	2	7	8	4

2 4 4

3	2	9	6	4	1	7	8	5
7	1	6	8	2	5	9	4	3
4	5	8	7	3	9	6	2	1
6	3	2	4	8	7	1	5	9
1	7	5	2	9	6	4	3	8
8	9	4	5	1	3	2	7	6
9	4	3	1	5	2	8	6	7
2	6	1	3	7	8	5	9	4
5	8	7	9	6	4	3	1	2

2 4 5

9	5	8	4	7	1	2	3	6
2	6	7	8	9	3	5	4	1
3	1	4	5	2	6	8	7	9
1	9	3	6	8	5	4	2	7
7	4	6	3	1	2	9	5	8
5	8	2	9	4	7	6	1	3
8	3	9	1	5	4	7	6	2
4	2	1	7	6	9	3	8	5
6	7	5	2	3	8	1	9	4

2 4 6

2	1	5	6	7	4	3	8	9
6	4	9	8	3	1	5	2	7
8	3	7	5	9	2	4	1	6
4	6	3	2	5	7	1	9	8
1	7	2	9	4	8	6	5	3
9	5	8	3	1	6	2	7	4
3	9	1	4	8	5	7	6	2
5	2	4	7	6	9	8	3	1
7	8	6	1	2	3	9	4	5

2 4 7

5	3	4	1	9	7	8	6	2
9	1	7	8	6	2	3	4	5
6	2	8	3	4	5	9	1	7
3	6	1	4	2	9	7	5	8
2	8	5	7	3	6	4	9	1
7	4	9	5	1	8	2	3	6
8	9	2	6	5	3	1	7	4
4	5	3	2	7	1	6	8	9
1	7	6	9	8	4	5	2	3

2 4 8

9	5	1	3	4	6	2	7	8
6	2	7	9	5	8	4	1	3
3	4	8	1	7	2	9	5	6
2	8	4	6	1	7	3	9	5
5	9	3	2	8	4	7	6	1
7	1	6	5	3	9	8	4	2
1	3	9	7	2	5	6	8	4
8	6	2	4	9	1	5	3	7
4	7	5	8	6	3	1	2	9

2 4 9

7	4	6	3	1	9	8	5	2
2	8	1	4	5	7	6	9	3
3	9	5	8	6	2	7	1	4
5	7	9	2	3	4	1	8	6
4	6	2	9	8	1	3	7	5
8	1	3	6	7	5	4	2	9
9	3	7	1	2	6	5	4	8
6	5	4	7	9	8	2	3	1
1	2	8	5	4	3	9	6	7

2 5 0

9	2	8	4	5	6	1	3	7
3	5	4	7	8	1	9	2	6
1	6	7	3	9	2	5	4	8
5	1	2	6	4	8	3	7	9
4	8	6	9	3	7	2	1	5
7	9	3	2	1	5	6	8	4
8	4	1	5	2	9	7	6	3
6	3	9	1	7	4	8	5	2
2	7	5	8	6	3	4	9	1

2 5 1

8	2	3	6	4	1	9	5	7
1	5	9	7	3	2	6	4	8
4	6	7	5	8	9	1	2	3
2	3	8	9	5	4	7	6	1
7	9	4	2	1	6	3	8	5
5	1	6	8	7	3	2	9	4
6	7	5	1	2	8	4	3	9
3	8	2	4	9	7	5	1	6
9	4	1	3	6	5	8	7	2

2 5 2

2	1	6	4	3	8	7	5	9
5	4	9	1	2	7	3	6	8
3	7	8	9	5	6	1	4	2
6	8	5	2	4	1	9	3	7
1	3	4	5	7	9	2	8	6
7	9	2	6	8	3	5	1	4
4	5	1	7	6	2	8	9	3
9	2	3	8	1	4	6	7	5
8	6	7	3	9	5	4	2	1

253

9	4	5	7	8	3	1	6	2
8	7	2	6	1	9	3	4	5
3	6	1	2	5	4	8	9	7
7	1	4	9	3	5	6	2	8
5	9	6	4	2	8	7	3	1
2	3	8	1	6	7	9	5	4
6	2	7	5	9	1	4	8	3
1	8	9	3	4	2	5	7	6
4	5	3	8	7	6	2	1	9

254

6	7	1	2	4	5	3	8	9
4	2	3	6	9	8	5	1	7
9	8	5	7	3	1	4	6	2
5	4	9	8	2	3	6	7	1
2	3	7	4	1	6	9	5	8
1	6	8	9	5	7	2	3	4
7	9	6	3	8	4	1	2	5
3	5	2	1	7	9	8	4	6
8	1	4	5	6	2	7	9	3

255

1	5	9	8	7	3	2	4	6
3	4	8	1	6	2	7	9	5
2	6	7	5	9	4	8	3	1
4	7	1	3	8	5	6	2	9
6	9	2	4	1	7	5	8	3
5	8	3	6	2	9	1	7	4
7	1	5	9	4	8	3	6	2
8	3	4	2	5	6	9	1	7
9	2	6	7	3	1	4	5	8

256

8	3	2	5	7	6	1	9	4
5	6	9	3	1	4	7	2	8
7	1	4	8	2	9	6	5	3
6	5	7	9	3	2	4	8	1
2	8	3	4	6	1	9	7	5
4	9	1	7	5	8	2	3	6
3	2	5	1	4	7	8	6	9
9	4	6	2	8	5	3	1	7
1	7	8	6	9	3	5	4	2

257

9	4	3	6	5	2	1	8	7
2	8	6	7	9	1	5	4	3
5	1	7	3	8	4	9	6	2
3	6	2	8	7	5	4	9	1
7	5	1	2	4	9	6	3	8
8	9	4	1	6	3	2	7	5
4	2	5	9	3	7	8	1	6
1	3	8	4	2	6	7	5	9
6	7	9	5	1	8	3	2	4

258

6	7	8	2	3	5	1	4	9
4	2	1	6	7	9	5	8	3
3	9	5	1	4	8	2	7	6
9	6	7	5	1	3	8	2	4
8	3	4	9	2	7	6	5	1
1	5	2	8	6	4	3	9	7
7	4	6	3	5	2	9	1	8
5	1	9	4	8	6	7	3	2
2	8	3	7	9	1	4	6	5

259

7	5	9	4	6	3	1	2	8
4	2	8	9	7	1	5	6	3
1	6	3	2	8	5	7	4	9
3	4	5	8	9	2	6	7	1
2	1	6	3	5	7	9	8	4
8	9	7	6	1	4	3	5	2
6	3	1	5	2	8	4	9	7
9	7	2	1	4	6	8	3	5
5	8	4	7	3	9	2	1	6

260

6	2	5	8	4	3	7	1	9
1	3	4	2	9	7	8	5	6
9	7	8	1	5	6	2	4	3
8	1	6	7	3	4	5	9	2
2	9	7	6	8	5	1	3	4
4	5	3	9	1	2	6	8	7
5	6	1	4	7	9	3	2	8
3	4	2	5	6	8	9	7	1
7	8	9	3	2	1	4	6	5

261

9	2	6	3	7	1	4	8	5
3	4	7	6	5	8	1	9	2
1	5	8	2	4	9	7	3	6
7	8	2	1	3	5	6	4	9
5	9	4	8	2	6	3	1	7
6	1	3	4	9	7	2	5	8
2	7	1	5	8	4	9	6	3
4	3	5	9	6	2	8	7	1
8	6	9	7	1	3	5	2	4

262

8	7	5	1	6	2	9	4	3
9	1	6	7	4	3	2	8	5
4	2	3	5	9	8	1	6	7
5	6	9	3	8	7	4	2	1
2	3	8	6	1	4	7	5	9
7	4	1	9	2	5	8	3	6
3	5	4	2	7	1	6	9	8
1	9	2	8	5	6	3	7	4
6	8	7	4	3	9	5	1	2

263

7	5	9	8	1	4	3	6	2
2	6	4	7	9	3	1	5	8
3	1	8	6	2	5	4	9	7
8	3	5	2	6	1	7	4	9
9	4	6	5	3	7	8	2	1
1	2	7	9	4	8	5	3	6
4	9	3	1	7	2	6	8	5
5	7	2	3	8	6	9	1	4
6	8	1	4	5	9	2	7	3

264

2	1	6	3	5	4	7	8	9
4	7	9	6	1	8	5	3	2
8	3	5	9	2	7	1	6	4
6	5	4	2	9	1	8	7	3
9	8	7	5	4	3	2	1	6
1	2	3	7	8	6	4	9	5
5	6	8	4	7	9	3	2	1
3	4	1	8	6	2	9	5	7
7	9	2	1	3	5	6	4	8

265

1	6	5	3	4	2	9	7	8
7	8	9	1	6	5	2	3	4
2	3	4	9	7	8	6	5	1
8	7	2	4	3	6	1	9	5
4	5	6	8	9	1	7	2	3
9	1	3	2	5	7	4	8	6
6	2	1	5	8	9	3	4	7
5	4	7	6	2	3	8	1	9
3	9	8	7	1	4	5	6	2

266

6	2	1	9	5	8	3	7	4
5	7	8	6	3	4	9	1	2
9	3	4	2	1	7	6	8	5
4	1	5	7	2	6	8	3	9
7	9	6	4	8	3	2	5	1
3	8	2	1	9	5	4	6	7
8	4	3	5	7	9	1	2	6
1	6	7	3	4	2	5	9	8
2	5	9	8	6	1	7	4	3

267

6	3	9	7	4	1	5	2	8
8	5	1	3	9	2	6	4	7
7	4	2	5	8	6	3	9	1
5	1	8	2	6	3	9	7	4
3	7	4	8	5	9	1	6	2
9	2	6	1	7	4	8	3	5
2	6	5	4	3	8	7	1	9
4	8	3	9	1	7	2	5	6
1	9	7	6	2	5	4	8	3

268

2	4	5	8	6	1	7	3	9
1	6	3	9	4	7	5	8	2
8	9	7	3	5	2	4	6	1
9	7	1	2	8	6	3	4	5
3	2	4	5	7	9	6	1	8
6	5	8	1	3	4	2	9	7
4	3	2	7	9	8	1	5	6
5	1	9	6	2	3	8	7	4
7	8	6	4	1	5	9	2	3

269

6	1	8	5	4	3	7	9	2
5	2	4	6	7	9	8	3	1
7	3	9	8	2	1	6	5	4
1	5	2	7	6	8	3	4	9
8	7	3	1	9	4	2	6	5
4	9	6	2	3	5	1	8	7
2	6	5	4	8	7	9	1	3
3	8	1	9	5	2	4	7	6
9	4	7	3	1	6	5	2	8

270

3	4	5	7	2	9	1	6	8
1	7	2	8	4	6	3	9	5
8	9	6	5	1	3	7	2	4
2	1	7	9	8	5	6	4	3
4	5	8	6	3	2	9	1	7
6	3	9	1	7	4	5	8	2
9	8	1	4	5	7	2	3	6
5	2	4	3	6	1	8	7	9
7	6	3	2	9	8	4	5	1